W9-BSY-868

COMFORT IN AN INSTANT

COMFORT IN AN INSTANT

75 COMFORT FOOD RECIPES FOR YOUR PRESSURE COOKER, MULTICOOKER + INSTANT POT®

MELISSA CLARK

CLARKSON POTTER/PUBLISHERS
NEW YORK

Published in the United States by Clarkson Potter/ Publishers, an imprint of the Crown Publishing Group, a division of Penguin Random House LLC, New York. clarksonpotter.com

CLARKSON POTTER is a trademark and POTTER with colophon is a registered trademark of Penguin Random House LLC.

Library of Congress Cataloging-in-Publication Data
Names: Clark, Melissa, author.
Title: Comfort in an instant: 75 comfort food recipes for your pressure cooker, multicooker, and Instant Pot / Melissa Clark.
Description: First edition. | New York: Clarkson Potter/Publishers, 2018.
Identifiers: LCCN 2018019955 (print) | LCCN 2018021152 (ebook) | ISBN 9780525576167 (ebook) | ISBN 9780525576150
Subjects: LCSH: Comfort food. | Pressure cooking. | LCGFT: Cookbooks.
Classification: LCC TX714 (ebook) | LCC TX714 .C5533 2018 (print) | DDC 641.5/87—dc23
LC record available at https://lccn.loc.gov/2018019955

ISBN 978-0-525-57615-0
Ebook ISBN 978-0-525-57616-7

Printed in Germany

Book and cover design by Marysarah Quinn
Photographs by Christopher Testani

10 9 8 7 6 5 4 3 2 1

FIRST EDITION

TO DAHLIA AND DANIEL,
WHO ARE A COMFORT TO ME
EVERY SINGLE DAY

CONTENTS

INTRODUCTION

A few years ago I was given the assignment from the *New York Times* Food section to explore why legions of passionate home cooks were falling hard for their electric pressure cookers. Was this gadget a mere fad? Or would it weave its way into the fabric of our kitchen and our lives?

The answer of course is the latter. Electric pressure cookers (also called multipots) are on the culinary upswing. Once you get the hang of it (and see pages 10 to 17 for a little help), they make getting dinner on the table a snap.

They've certainly made my life easier. After using mine regularly for the past few years, there are some things—beans, braised meats, artichokes, bone broth, and brown rice—that I'd be absolutely bitter about having to go back to cooking in a pot on the stove. But with two multipots at the ready, I doubt I ever will.

Here, I include only recipes that show off what the machines excel at—not so much what they *can* do, but what they can do as well or better than traditional methods, be it faster, more flavorfully, or more conveniently. The key to pressure-cooker success is choosing recipes in which softness and succulence is the goal, and which traditionally take hours to get there. An electric pressure cooker can't cook a whole chicken very well, and it doesn't do crisp or crunchy. So if you don't ask it to do what it can't, you won't be disappointed.

Instead, use it to make comforting dishes like turkey meatloaf spiked with Sriracha and served on a mound of buttered potatoes (page 74), or cumin-scented Cuban chicken and rice (page 63) on any given weekday. Cooking spaghetti and meatballs (page 46) in a multipot may seem counterintuitive, but the appliance makes a rather labor-intensive process perfect for a family-friendly after-work meal. And on weekends when you've got more time, try my take on David Chang's Bo Ssam (page 100), a Korean dish of marinated pork shoulder; I pressure cook it until spoonably tender, and then broil it until it's a glisteningly caramelized vision.

There is, however, one thing to bear in mind with all multipots: Although the pioneering brand in the category is called the Instant Pot, you shouldn't expect instantaneous meals. Faster, more convenient, and tasty meals, yes. But be prepared for the lag time it takes for the machine to reach and release pressure—10 to 30 minutes—as well as the usual prep time of cooking. That is why, for example, the luscious Lemon Chicken with Garlic and Olives on page 65 calls for a pressure-cook time of only 15 minutes, but the total time is closer to 45 minutes. It's still much faster than using a traditional oven, but by no means "instant." Read the title of this book with a knowing wink.

That said, in putting together this collection, I did make sure to include over fifty of my favorite recipes that could be put together in under an hour: 50 under 60, as it were. Even better, most of that time is hands off. Throw everything in the machine and go for a run. Or have a glass of wine and help your kids with their homework. Dinner will be ready when you are.

GETTING TO KNOW YOUR ELECTRIC PRESSURE COOKER

If you're an old hand at cooking with pressure cookers, you can skip this section. And, if you've read my first electric pressure cooker book, *Dinner in an Instant,* you can also skip this section, as the information is the same. Many new electric pressure cooker brands and models have hit the market since that book's publication, but the fundamentals are unchanged. Novices, however, should read on for some crucial information that will help you avoid the pitfalls and get comfortable with all the functions of your device.

Most electric pressure cookers are also multipurpose cookers, or multipots, meaning they can do many things beyond just cooking under pressure. Most models can steam, sauté, slow-cook, pressure-cook, and even make yogurt.

The pressure function is one of the handiest because cooking foods at a lower temperature but higher pressure allows for a faster cooking time than you would need on the stove or in the oven. It lets you achieve certain shortcuts, like cooking dried beans without soaking them first or cooking polenta without stirring. And it is amazing

for braising meats, which never dry out and always cook up tender and luscious.

Because I'm always in a rush, and assume you usually are too, I've written most of these recipes to use the pressure cooker function whenever possible. But whenever the results are equally good using the slow cooker function, I have included directions for that as well (see "Cook It Slow" at the end of some of the recipes). This gives you options. Because sometimes you do need to slow things down to make them fit most easily into your schedule.

These recipes will work in any electric pressure cooker on the market. In terms of developing the recipes, I tested them using three popular brands: Instant Pot, Breville, and Fagor, and found them all more or less the same in terms of functionality. They all cooked the ingredients pretty similarly. The differences were in their designs. Some models were more intuitive for me to use than others. This, however, is entirely subjective.

WHAT SIZE PRESSURE COOKER SHOULD I BUY?

This is one of my more frequently asked questions. I currently own two electric pressure cookers: a 6-quart that I use for most of my daily cooking, and an 8-quart I'll pull out when I make my biweekly batch of bone broth or other stocks or large batches of soup or stew.

I generally recommend the 6-quart model as the best size for most families, though if you're often feeding a crowd, the 8-quart might be better for you. And if space is tight, you can make many of the recipes in this book in the 3-quart model, as long as you are careful never to fill the basin higher than the maximum fill line indicates (see page 17 for more information).

A NOTE ON THE BURN INDICATOR

There is some variation with different multipot brands and models, and one place that is very apparent is with the burn indicator light. I've never had mine go off but have heard reports that in other models, the burn indicator lights up and the machine turns itself off mid-recipe. While this is annoying, it's nothing to worry about. The fact is, your electric pressure cooker can't tell the difference between gorgeously caramelized and unappetizingly burnt. If your machine turns itself off mid-recipe, simply release the pressure, open it up, and add a tablespoon or two of water. Then turn it back on. That should fix the problem, and it shouldn't affect the outcome.

A NOTE ON ADDING LIQUID

If you've read your instruction manual, you may have noticed that it calls for adding a minimum amount of liquid to the pot—anywhere from ½ cup to 1½ cups, depending on the brand. In many cases, I don't do this because adding liquid to the pot is not always necessary. While it's true that a certain amount of liquid is necessary in order to create pressure, often a few tablespoons is enough to get the job done. Or sometimes, the moisture already present in the ingredients themselves achieves this goal—especially in watery ingredients such as fish and many vegetables. Always follow the recipe the first time to get your bearings, then feel free to go rogue.

A NOTE ON TIMING

Calculating the timing for the recipes in this book is not an exact science. To come up with the total time, I simply set a timer when I started cooking, then turned it off when the dish was completely done (rounding up to the nearest 5-minute interval). But it might take you slightly more or less time, depending on your model of multipot and your skill level with a knife. Use the times as a general guide rather than a strict set of parameters.

PRESSURE COOKER PARTS

It's imperative that you read the manual for your electric pressure cooker before you use it the first time, because the brands vary a bit. However, most pressure cookers come with the following parts:

- **Lid with steam valve and pressure valve**
- **Outer body**
- **Inner pot**
- **Steamer rack or basket**
- **Condensation reservoir** (for condensation during slow cooking; it attaches at the side of the lid once it's closed)

About the steam valve: This valve allows the pressure cooker to either build pressure or release it. It has a sealing (locked) position and a venting (open) position. When pressure-cooking, the valve must be in the sealing position. (Consult your manual if your valve looks different or has other options.)

The biggest mistake multipot novices make is not sealing (locking) the steam valve when attempting to use the pressure-cook function. In some multipot brands, you can't turn on the pressure cooker setting unless the steam valve is sealed, and this is an excellent thing. But in other brands—including the Instant Pot—you can. Thus, you will *think* the machine is building pressure, but it's not, because the steam valve is open and releasing steam. Everyone I know, myself included, makes this mistake at least once. You'll open your pot of beef stew or beans to find the meat tough instead of melting, the beans crunchy instead of velvety. So double- and triple-check to make sure the valve is sealed, and if you find that something you made comes out underdone, this is probably the reason why.

About the pressure valve: This metal valve indicates when the cooker is pressurized and when it is not. When the cooker reaches pressure, it will pop up. When the pressure is released, it will drop down. In some models, the valve might be hidden underneath a cover. But it's there doing its job whether you see it or not.

MULTICOOKER FUNCTIONS

Sauté: The sauté function works like a burner on your stove, heating the inner pot from the bottom up and allowing you to brown meats and vegetables and to simmer sauces to reduce them. The sauté function on most cookers has several levels, from low to high (check your manual to find out), so you can adjust the heat. If yours doesn't, and if at some point the pot seems too hot and the food is turning too dark too quickly, simply turn the machine off for a few minutes to bring the heat down. Then turn it back on if necessary. It's not a perfect solution but it works well enough, and the pot will adjust to the temperature change (on or off) fairly quickly. Or you can always brown the ingredients in a skillet on top of the stove and then transfer them to the pot for the remainder of the cooking. Note that when sautéing, the lid of the pressure cooker should always be off.

Pressure Cook: There are two options for pressure cooking: high and low. Check the recipe and set the cooker for the correct pressure level, then set the length of time you'd like the ingredients to cook. High pressure is used for most recipes, with low pressure appropriate for more delicate ingredients, like seafood, custards, some vegetables, and eggs.

Slow Cook: If you have already used a Crock-Pot or other slow cooker, this will be familiar to you: The slow cooker function on your multicooker cooks your food very, very slowly. You may have the option to cook it at either a high or low setting, depending on your model. Some models provide a separate clear glass cover so you can monitor the food as it is slow-cooking. Other models will have you lock the lid on as if you were going to pressure-cook the dish—except, crucially, the steam valve remains open so the steam can vent. And you can take the top off to check on things as they cook.

Yogurt: The use of this function will vary based on the recipe and your model. Most yogurt functions will heat the pot to between 180° and 200°F, which is the temperature needed for the milk to thicken, then reduce the temperature to 110°F for fermentation time. The nice thing about the yogurt function is that you don't have to worry about the milk burning or bubbling over, and you can be sure it always reaches the correct temperature. Nor do you have to worry about finding a warm but not too warm spot for the yogurt to ferment. The multipot takes care of that for you. Consult your manual for exact instructions.

WHAT YOU'RE GOING TO NEED FOR THESE RECIPES

- **Aluminum foil,** for covering pans and for making slings (see page 17)
- **Metal springform cake pan:** 6- or 7-inch (never put any glass cookware in the multicooker)
- **Soufflé dish (porcelain):** 1-quart dish and 1½- or 2-quart dish (all about 7 inches in diameter)
- **Ramekins (porcelain):** 4 to 6 ounces each
- **Variety of steamer baskets and steamer racks:** Most pressure cookers will come with at least one steamer rack. This sits at the bottom of the cooker, usually over water or some kind of liquid. Some racks have attached metal handles, which allow you to lower and lift soufflé dishes and cake pans from the pot without tipping the dish. You'll want at least one steamer rack; if yours does not have a handle, you can simply make a foil sling to help you lower it into, and lift it up from, the pot (see page 17).

I'd also advise you to get at least one steamer basket. Different from a rack, this contraption has short legs and a basket-like top with a handle. It's handy for lifting a lot of small things out of the pressure cooker at one time—potatoes, for example—which would roll off a flat steamer rack.

NOTES FOR PRESSURE COOKING: MANUAL VERSUS NATURAL RELEASE

- When the pressure-cooking time is up, the cooker will automatically change to the "keep warm" function and begin to gradually lose pressure. It can take as long as 30 minutes to release naturally on its own. If the recipe calls for an immediate manual release, turn the steam valve to its venting position when the cook time is complete. Take care to keep your hand away from the valve (not above it) so as not to burn yourself when the rush of hot steam blasts forth. Some people like to turn the valve with the handle of a wooden spoon. Or consider covering the valve with a dish towel before opening it, which has the added bonus of keeping the steam from spraying all over your kitchen.
- Note that if a recipe calls for a manual pressure release, it's important to do as suggested as soon as the machine beeps (or set a timer if you're going to be in another room). Otherwise, the food inside might overcook.
- Some recipes call for a specific time for natural release before manually releasing the rest of the pressure. In that case, turn off the pot if it doesn't turn itself off, but do not release the valve until the natural release time has passed. Then open the steam valve to release the rest of the pressure. This allows the food to continue to cook a little longer than with a straight manual release, but without the pot being on full pressure for that whole time. It's a slightly gentler and slower cooking environment.
- The time for a full natural release varies (usually between 10 and 20 minutes, but it can be longer). The longer the pressure cooker has been on and the fuller it is, the longer the natural release will take. On most models you will know that all the pressure has released naturally when the pressure valve drops down and the lid is unlocked.

A note on reaching pressure: When you select pressure cooking and set a time, the clock will not immediately begin to count down. This is because the pot must first build pressure before it starts to cook. This can take anywhere from 3 to 10 minutes, depending upon the contents of the pot. Always double-check that the steam valve is in the locked, sealing position. Pressure cannot build if it is venting.

A note on pressure cooking versus slow cooking: In this book, I include the cook time for both pressure cooking and slow cooking when applicable. The initial directions will be those for pressure cooking. Following the recipe, there will be directions for "Cook It Slow." If you prefer to cook a dish all day long or overnight, the slow-cooking option will be useful for you.

AIDS FOR LOWERING AND LIFTING

- If your steamer rack does not have handles, it's easy to build a sling that will help you lift soufflé dishes and cake pans out of the cooker. To make one, fold a long piece (about 16 inches) of aluminum foil into thirds so that it can sit under the dish or pan and extend up the sides of the pressure cooker pot (as handles). This will help you lift and lower the dish or pan from the cooker. Be sure to leave the sling in the machine while cooking so you can use it to lift the dish out afterward. Note that it will be hot after cooking, so use oven mitts.

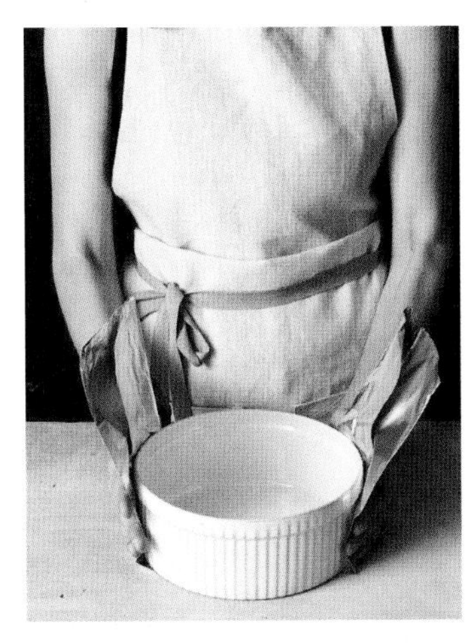

- Tongs are helpful for lifting out small hot pans, ramekins, or dishes. I usually use them in one hand with oven mitt on the other hand.

MORE TIPS

- Lock the steam valve before pressure cooking. Pressure will never build if the valve is turned to venting.
- The steam valve should NOT be locked when steaming, slow cooking, or using the yogurt function. The entire lid should be off when sautéing.
- Don't fill the pot more than two-thirds full with any liquid or stew. Keep in mind that some foods expand, such as rice or oats.
- The condensation collector should be attached for slow cooking to prevent water from leaking onto your counter.
- Always cover cake pans and soufflé dishes with aluminum foil when cooking under pressure. Without the foil, condensation will collect in the dishes and water down the food, in some cases ruining it (puddings and custards, for example).
- To avoid being burned and to avoid having your kitchen fill with steam, you can put a dish towel over the steamer valve before releasing the pressure manually. Do not hold your hands directly over the steam valve.
- Be aware that when the lid is removed after the pressure is released, there will be some excess water clinging to it. Turn the lid outward and away from you, so that the condensation does not drip back into the pot.
- If something comes out undercooked, re-cover the pot, lock the steam valve, re-pressurize, and cook again for an extra few minutes (depending on how much more time you think the dish needs). If the recipe initially called for a natural release, release it naturally again.

COMFORTING MORNINGS

BREAKFAST POLENTA WITH DRIED APRICOTS + CINNAMON

ACTIVE TIME: 5 MINUTES
PRESSURE COOK TIME: 22 MINUTES
TOTAL TIME: 50 MINUTES
YIELD: 4 SERVINGS

1¼ cups whole milk

¾ cup coarse or medium polenta or cornmeal

¼ cup diced dried apricots

1 cinnamon stick

¼ teaspoon fine sea salt

2 tablespoons unsalted butter, cubed

Ground cinnamon, for serving

Demerara or turbinado sugar, for serving

Flaky sea salt, for serving

Breakfast polenta (which was always called cornmeal mush in those Laura Ingalls Wilder books of my youth) is a sweet and sunshine-colored alternative to the usual porridge. This version, cooked in whole milk for richness, is scented with cinnamon and studded with chewy dried apricots—though feel free to leave them out or substitute another dried fruit such as raisins or diced prunes. I like to top my bowl with a knob of salty butter and a drizzle of heavy cream, but yogurt is also nice here, adding a pleasing tang.

---

1. Pour 1 cup water into the pressure cooker pot.

2. In a medium metal bowl (not glass or plastic) that will fit in the pressure cooker pot, stir together ¼ cup water, the milk, polenta, apricots, cinnamon stick, salt, and 1 tablespoon of the butter.

3. If your steamer rack has handles, place the bowl on the rack and lower everything into the pressure cooker pot. If your rack does not have handles, first place the rack in the pot, then lower in the bowl using a homemade sling (see page 17). Do not put the bowl directly into the pot without a rack/trivet; it should sit above, not in, the water.

4. Lock the lid into place and cook on high pressure for 22 minutes. Let the pressure release naturally.

5. Carefully remove the bowl from the pressure cooker, using the sling or oven mitts. Stir the remaining 1 tablespoon butter into the polenta. If it seems too thick, stir in some more water or milk.

6. To serve, remove the cinnamon stick and spoon the polenta into bowls. Top with a sprinkling of cinnamon, demerara sugar, and flaky sea salt.

COOK IT SLOW

Cook on high for 1 to 2 hours or low for 4 to 5 hours. Give it a stir about halfway through the cooking process.

QUINOA PORRIDGE WITH BROWN BUTTER ALMONDS

ACTIVE TIME: 10 MINUTES
PRESSURE COOK TIME: 2 MINUTES
TOTAL TIME: 40 MINUTES
YIELD: 4 SERVINGS

---

2 tablespoons unsalted butter

¼ cup sliced almonds

1 cup quinoa, rinsed very well in warm water

2½ cups almond milk (or your milk of choice)

Pinch of salt

Maple syrup, for serving

Berries, for serving (optional)

COOK IT SLOW

Cook on high for 4 to 5 hours or low for 7 to 8 hours.

High-protein quinoa is a perfect food to start your day, especially when cooked in almond milk and topped with brown butter almonds. Be sure to rinse your quinoa very well before cooking (I use a fine sieve for this). This helps remove its natural bitterness, making for a sweeter, gentler porridge.

---

1. Using the sauté function, melt the butter in the pressure cooker pot, letting it heat until it turns dark golden brown and smells nutty, 3 to 7 minutes. Add the almonds and cook until golden at the edges, 1 to 2 minutes more. Using a spoon, scoop the almonds and as much of the butter from the pot as possible into a small bowl to save for garnish.

2. Add the rinsed quinoa, almond milk, and salt to the pot.

3. Lock the lid into place and cook on high pressure for 2 minutes. Let the pressure release naturally for 10 minutes, then manually release the remaining pressure.

4. Use a fork to fluff the quinoa, then serve topped with the almonds and brown butter, a drizzle of maple syrup, and berries, if you like.

GOAT CHEESE + MUSHROOM FRITTATA

ACTIVE TIME: 15 MINUTES
PRESSURE COOK TIME: 25 MINUTES
TOTAL TIME: 55 MINUTES
YIELD: 4 SERVINGS

---

1 tablespoon unsalted butter, plus more for the soufflé dish

5 tablespoons grated Parmesan cheese

1 tablespoon extra-virgin olive oil

8 ounces cremini or white mushrooms, thinly sliced

2 garlic cloves, minced

2 tablespoons finely chopped fresh sage

2 teaspoons finely chopped fresh thyme

1 teaspoon kosher salt

9 large eggs

½ cup whole milk

2 tablespoons all-purpose flour

¼ teaspoon freshly ground black pepper

3 ounces soft goat cheese

Goat cheese and sautéed mushrooms make this frittata deeply flavorful, and cooking it in an electric pressure cooker makes it convenient because you don't have to keep an eye on it. If you're not a goat cheese fan, you can substitute grated Gruyère, cheddar, or even cubes of Brie.

---

1. Butter a porcelain or ceramic (not glass) 7-inch soufflé dish and dust the sides with 2 tablespoons of the Parmesan. Set aside.

2. Using the sauté function, melt the 1 tablespoon butter and the oil in the pressure cooker pot. Add the mushrooms and cook, stirring occasionally, until browned, about 7 minutes. Stir in the garlic, sage, and thyme and cook until the mushrooms are tender, another 2 minutes. Scrape into a small bowl, sprinkle with ¼ teaspoon of the salt, and set aside until cool, 3 to 5 minutes.

3. In a large bowl, whisk together the eggs, milk, flour, pepper, and the remaining ¾ teaspoon salt. Stir in the cooled mushrooms and goat cheese, then scrape into the prepared soufflé dish. Cover the dish with aluminum foil.

4. Pour 1½ cups water into the pressure cooker (no need to wash it out first). If your steamer rack has handles, place the soufflé dish on the rack and lower everything into the pressure cooker pot. If your rack does not have handles, first place the rack in the pot, then lower in the soufflé dish using a homemade sling (see page 17).

5. Lock the lid into place and cook on high pressure for 25 minutes. Let the pressure release naturally for 10 minutes, then manually release the remaining pressure. Carefully remove the dish from the pressure cooker, using the sling or oven mitts. Remove the foil.

6. Heat the broiler. Sprinkle the remaining 3 tablespoons Parmesan cheese over the frittata, then broil until it is golden brown, 2 to 3 minutes. Let it sit for 5 minutes before serving.

CARAMELIZED SWEET POTATOES, ONIONS + EGGS

ACTIVE TIME: 15 MINUTES
PRESSURE COOK TIME: 3 MINUTES
TOTAL TIME: 35 MINUTES
YIELD: 2 TO 4 SERVINGS

1½ pounds sweet potatoes, peeled and cut into ¾-inch cubes

2 tablespoons unsalted butter, melted

3 tablespoons extra-virgin olive oil

1 small onion, diced

1 serrano chile, diced

2 garlic cloves, minced

¾ teaspoon kosher salt

½ teaspoon sweet paprika

4 large eggs

Chopped chives, for serving

Hot sauce, such as harissa, Sriracha, or Tabasco, for serving

---

In this cozy breakfast or brunch dish, sweet potatoes are pressure-cooked until velvety tender, then browned in butter with onion, green chile, and garlic before being topped with runny-yolked eggs. It's a bit like hash, though soft and caramelized instead of crisp.

---

1. Pour ½ cup water into the pressure cooker pot. Set a steamer basket in the bottom and fill it with the sweet potatoes.

2. Lock the lid into place and cook on high pressure for 3 minutes. Manually release the pressure.

3. Remove the steamer basket with the potatoes. Drain the water from the pot and wipe it out so it's dry.

4. Using the sauté function set on high, if possible, melt the butter and 2 tablespoons of the oil. Stir in the onion, serrano, garlic, and ¼ teaspoon of the salt. Cook until translucent and just starting to brown, about 5 minutes. Stir in the remaining ½ teaspoon salt, the paprika, and cooked sweet potatoes and spread out in an even layer on the bottom of the pot. Drizzle the remaining 1 tablespoon oil over the potatoes.

5. Crack the eggs over the sweet potato mixture, and place the cover on the pot (you don't need to lock the lid into place). Let everything continue to cook until the eggs are just set, but the yolks are still runny, about 4 minutes.

6. Turn off the sauté function and let the hash sit for 5 minutes. To serve, scoop the sweet potatoes and eggs out and transfer to serving plates, making sure to get the caramelized bits on the bottom of the pot. Top with chopped chives and serve with hot sauce.

CHEDDAR-SPINACH STRATA

ACTIVE TIME: 20 MINUTES
PRESSURE COOK TIME: 25 MINUTES
TOTAL TIME: 1 HOUR 15 MINUTES
YIELD: 4 SERVINGS

---

1 tablespoon unsalted butter

1 small red onion, diced

4 cups baby spinach (5 ounces)

¼ cup chopped fresh basil, plus more for garnish

1 fat garlic clove, finely grated or minced

½ teaspoon kosher salt, plus more as needed

3 large eggs

1½ cups whole milk

½ cup grated extra-sharp cheddar cheese

½ teaspoon Tabasco sauce, plus more for serving

¼ teaspoon freshly ground black pepper

⅛ teaspoon freshly grated nutmeg

2 cups dry white country bread or baguette cubes, in 1-inch pieces

---

Essentially a cheesy, savory bread pudding, this strata has enough vegetable matter—thanks to the baby spinach—to offset the richness of the cheddar. Make sure to use a nice, extra-sharp cheese here; its tang makes a great contrast to all the milk and eggs. Serve this still warm from the oven when the cheese is still a little runny. I like to save left-over bread in a plastic bag in the freezer, and when I have enough, I'll make a strata.

---

1. Using the sauté function, melt the butter in the pressure cooker pot. Stir in the onion and sauté until golden brown at the edges, about 3 minutes.

2. Add the spinach, basil, garlic, and ¼ teaspoon of the salt and sauté until the spinach wilts and its liquid cooks off, about 3 minutes more. Taste and add more salt if needed.

3. In a medium bowl, whisk together the eggs, milk, ¼ cup of the cheddar, the Tabasco, pepper, nutmeg, and remaining ¼ teaspoon salt. Toss in the bread, then the spinach/onion mixture. Pour the bread and custard mixture into a porcelain or ceramic (not glass) 7-inch 1½-quart soufflé dish. Cover the dish with aluminum foil.

4. Pour 2 cups water into the pressure cooker pot (no need to rinse it out first). If your steamer rack has handles, place the soufflé dish on the rack and lower everything into the pressure cooker pot. If your rack does not have handles, first place the rack in the pot, then lower in the dish using a homemade sling (see page 17).

5. Lock the lid into place and cook on low pressure for 25 minutes. Let the pressure release naturally. Carefully remove the dish from the pressure cooker, using the sling or oven mitts.

6. Heat the broiler. Uncover the soufflé dish and place on a small rimmed baking sheet. Sprinkle with the remaining ¼ cup cheddar. Broil until the top is golden, 30 seconds to 1 minute. Serve warm, with Tabasco sauce to taste, and garnished with chopped basil, if you like.

CHEDDAR-SPINACH STRATA

NUTTY CHOCOLATE OATMEAL

ACTIVE TIME: 5 MINUTES
PRESSURE COOK TIME: 9 MINUTES
TOTAL TIME: 35 MINUTES
YIELD: 2 TO 3 SERVINGS

1 cup steel-cut oats

2 tablespoons unsweetened cocoa powder, preferably Dutch process

Pinch of sea salt

2 to 4 tablespoons nut butter (peanut, almond, or hazelnut are all great here), to taste

Demerara sugar, coconut sugar, or light brown sugar

Heavy cream, nut milk, or full-fat coconut milk, for garnish (optional)

Flaky sea salt, for garnish (optional)

COOK IT SLOW

Cook on high for 5 to 7 hours or low for 8 to 10 hours.

Chocolate oatmeal may sound like dessert, but it is completely breakfast worthy given the antioxidant content of unsweetened cocoa powder (which also happens to be naturally low in fat). Add a dollop of protein-rich nut butter to the bowl and you've got a satisfying breakfast that only feels like a decadent treat.

1. In the pressure cooker pot, whisk together 3 cups water, the oats, cocoa powder, and salt until all the cocoa powder lumps are dissolved.

2. Lock the lid into place and cook on high pressure for 9 minutes. Let the pressure release naturally for 10 minutes, then manually release the remaining pressure.

3. Stir up the oatmeal, then stir in the nut butter and sugar to taste. Garnish with cream, nut milk, or coconut milk, and a sprinkle of flaky salt if you like.

SAVORY SAUSAGE + BROCCOLI BREAD PUDDING

ACTIVE TIME: 20 MINUTES
PRESSURE COOK TIME: 25 MINUTES
TOTAL TIME: 1 HOUR 15 MINUTES
YIELD: 4 TO 6 SERVINGS

---

2 tablespoons extra-virgin olive oil

6 ounces sweet or spicy Italian sausage (pork or turkey), casings removed

1 small yellow onion, diced

1 cup diced (½-inch pieces) broccoli (6 ounces)

2 teaspoons chopped fresh rosemary

½ teaspoon kosher salt, plus more as needed

3 large eggs

1½ cups whole milk

¼ cup chopped fresh parsley

1 garlic clove, finely grated or minced

1 teaspoon Worcestershire sauce

¼ teaspoon freshly ground black pepper

Large pinch of freshly grated nutmeg

2 cups dry white bread cubes (1-inch pieces)

¼ cup grated pecorino or Parmesan cheese

I love this meaty bread pudding for breakfast served with a fried egg on top. But it is equally good as a side dish to simple grilled or roasted chicken—a little like a baked stuffing casserole. If you're not a broccoli fan, zucchini or corn kernels make for a lovely, summery substitute.

---

1. Using the sauté function (on low, if possible), heat 1 tablespoon of the oil in the pressure cooker pot. Add the sausage and cook until browned, 7 to 10 minutes, using a wooden spoon to break it up, scraping up the browned bits as it cooks. Transfer the meat to a bowl.

2. Add the remaining 1 tablespoon oil to the pot. Stir in the onion, broccoli, rosemary, and ¼ teaspoon salt. Cook until the onion starts to brown, about 5 minutes. Taste and add more salt if needed. Scrape into the bowl with the sausage.

3. In a medium bowl, whisk together the eggs, milk, parsley, garlic, Worcestershire, pepper, nutmeg, and remaining ¼ teaspoon salt. Toss in the bread, then the sausage/broccoli/onion mixture. Pour the bread and custard mixture into a porcelain or ceramic (not glass), 7-inch 1½-quart soufflé dish. Cover the dish with aluminum foil.

4. Pour 2 cups water into the pressure cooker pot (no need to rinse it out first). If your steamer rack has handles, place the soufflé dish on the rack and lower everything into the pressure cooker pot. If your rack does not have handles, first place the rack in the pot, then lower in the soufflé dish using a homemade sling (see page 17).

5. Lock the lid into place and cook on low pressure for 25 minutes. Let the pressure release naturally for 10 minutes, then manually release the remaining pressure.

6. Heat the broiler. Carefully remove the soufflé dish from the pressure cooker, using the sling or oven mitts. Place on a small baking sheet. Sprinkle with the pecorino. Broil until the top is golden, 30 seconds to 1 minute.

BAKED EGGS + TOMATO CHEESE GRITS

ACTIVE TIME: 20 MINUTES
PRESSURE COOK TIME: 10 MINUTES
TOTAL TIME: 45 MINUTES
YIELD: 4 SERVINGS

Cubes of tomato give cheese grits a lighter and more savory character, which goes really well with the runny egg yolks on top. Serve this with a vinegary hot sauce on the side; I like Tabasco, but any brand you love will work.

---

3 tablespoons unsalted butter

1 tablespoon extra-virgin olive oil

1 cup old-fashioned or stone-ground grits

1 14.5-ounce can diced tomatoes

1½ teaspoons kosher salt

¼ teaspoon freshly ground black pepper

½ cup half-and-half or whole milk, or more to taste

1½ cups shredded cheddar cheese (6 ounces)

Tabasco or other hot sauce

4 large eggs

Sliced scallions, for serving

---

1. Using the sauté function, melt 1 tablespoon of the butter and the oil in the pressure cooker pot. Add the grits and cook, stirring occasionally, until toasted, about 3 minutes.

2. Stir in 1¼ cups water, the tomatoes, salt, and pepper. Lock the lid into place and cook on high pressure for 10 minutes. Let the pressure release naturally for 10 minutes, then manually release the remaining pressure.

3. Using the sauté function (set to low, if possible), stir the milk, cheddar, and remaining 2 tablespoons butter into the grits. Add Tabasco sauce to taste. Adjust the seasonings if necessary.

4. Immediately, while the grits are still steaming hot, make 4 divots in them, then crack in the eggs. (If the grits have cooled down, turn on the sauté function and reheat them, stirring, before adding the eggs.) Cover the pot (but do not lock on the lid) and let the eggs cook in the residual heat of the pot until they are set to taste, 3 minutes for very runny eggs, 4 to 5 minutes for firmer eggs. Serve immediately, with more hot sauce and scallions sprinkled on top.

FAST WEEKNIGHT COMFORT

PASTAS, GRAINS + LENTILS

ACEITE DE OLIVA
ECO
ORGANIC
BIO
1 CUP

MIDDLE EASTERN LENTILS + RICE WITH LEEKS + SPINACH

ACTIVE TIME: 15 MINUTES
PRESSURE COOK TIME: 9 MINUTES
TOTAL TIME: 50 MINUTES
YIELD: 4 TO 6 SERVINGS

---

3 tablespoons extra-virgin olive oil, plus more for serving

2 large or 3 small leeks (white and light green parts only), halved and thinly sliced

Kosher salt

2 garlic cloves, finely grated or minced

1 teaspoon ground cumin

¼ teaspoon ground allspice

⅛ teaspoon cayenne pepper

1 cup brown or green lentils

1 bay leaf

1 cinnamon stick

¾ cup long-grain white rice

5 ounces baby spinach

1 cup plain yogurt

Based on a Middle Eastern *mujaddara*, a homey mix of spiced simmered lentils and rice, this easy, meatless dish is rich with allspice, cinnamon, and sweet browned leeks. The handful of baby spinach stirred in toward the end turns it into a one-pot meal, and adds a bit of welcome color, too. If you don't have leeks, use an onion or two instead.

---

1. Using the sauté function, heat the oil in the pressure cooker pot. Stir in the leeks and cook, stirring occasionally, until they are dark golden at the edges, about 10 minutes. Season with a pinch of salt. Use a slotted spoon to scoop out half the leeks and transfer to a bowl; set aside for the garnish.

2. Stir the garlic into the pot and cook until fragrant, about 15 seconds. Stir in the cumin, allspice, and cayenne and cook for 30 seconds.

3. Add the lentils, 2¾ cups water, 2 teaspoons salt, the bay leaf, and cinnamon stick to the pot.

4. Lock the lid into place and cook on high pressure for 1 minute. Let the pressure release naturally for 5 minutes, then manually release the remaining pressure.

5. Uncover the pot and stir in the rice, working quickly so the lentil mixture stays hot. Lock the lid back into place and cook on high pressure for 8 minutes. Manually release the pressure.

6. Uncover and stir in the spinach. Cover the pot with the lid (but don't lock it on) and let it sit for 5 to 10 minutes to wilt the greens and finish cooking the rice.

7. In a small bowl, season the yogurt with salt to taste.

8. Discard the bay leaf and cinnamon stick. Serve the lentils warm, garnished with the reserved leeks and salted yogurt on top, and drizzled with more olive oil.

PIMIENTO MAC + CHEESE

ANCHOVY LOVER'S ORECCHIETTE WITH FENNEL + ONIONS

ACTIVE TIME: 35 MINUTES
PRESSURE COOK TIME: 5 MINUTES
TOTAL TIME: 50 MINUTES
YIELD: 3 TO 4 SERVINGS

---

2 tablespoons unsalted butter

4 tablespoons extra-virgin olive oil, plus more for drizzling

1 medium fennel bulb, trimmed and diced (fronds reserved for serving)

Kosher salt

1 large onion, diced

6 ounces anchovy fillets, preferably packed in olive oil, drained and minced

4 garlic cloves, finely grated or minced

¼ teaspoon freshly ground black pepper, plus more for serving

¼ teaspoon crushed red pepper flakes

16 ounces orecchiette

2 cups chicken stock or vegetable broth, preferably homemade (page 108)

Finely grated zest of 1 lemon

Fresh lemon juice, for serving

Fennel fronds or chopped chives, for serving

Freshly grated Parmesan cheese, for serving

The fennel and onions are sweet and caramelized, the anchovies briny and savory, and the lemon bright and fresh. Cooked all together, they make a complex sauce for orecchiette pasta. Note that this recipe calls for 6 ounces of anchovies, which may seem like an absurdly large amount. But it works—the little fish dissolve into a pungent sauce as they heat under pressure, and buttery pasta softens their salty bite. Use the best-quality anchovies here—usually those packed in olive oil in a glass jar where you can see the fillets are a good bet. Once taken out of the jar, good-quality anchovies should be firm and meaty, not mushy or gritty. Then take a bite; if one doesn't taste delicious, a sauce with two dozen or so of them won't either.

---

1. Using the sauté function, melt the butter and 2 tablespoons of the oil in the pressure cooker pot. Stir in the fennel and a large pinch of salt and cook until lightly browned, about 10 minutes.

2. Stir in the remaining 2 tablespoons oil, the onion, anchovies, garlic, black pepper, and red pepper flakes. Cook, stirring frequently with a wooden spatula or spoon to scrape up the browned bits on the bottom, until everything is caramelized, 15 to 20 minutes. If the bottom starts to burn, either turn the sauté function to low (if possible) or remove the pot from the pressure cooker to let it cool slightly.

3. Stir in the orecchiette, chicken stock or vegetable broth, 1½ cups water, the lemon zest, and ½ teaspoon salt. Lock the lid into place and cook on low pressure for 5 minutes. Manually release the pressure.

4. Stir the pasta and test for doneness—if it's too al dente, cover the pot with the lid (but don't lock it on), and let it sit for 5 minutes to cook the pasta a little more.

5. To serve, scoop the pasta into serving bowls, then drizzle with oil and lemon juice. Top with fennel fronds, black pepper, and a generous amount of Parmesan.

POTATO, CAULIFLOWER + PEA CURRY

ACTIVE TIME: 15 MINUTES
PRESSURE COOK TIME: 8 MINUTES
TOTAL TIME: 35 MINUTES
YIELD: 4 SERVINGS

¼ cup peanut or safflower oil

1½ teaspoons cumin seeds

1¾ pounds white or gold potatoes, peeled if you like, cut into ¼-inch-thick slices

1 green chile, such as jalapeño, seeded if desired, thinly sliced

1 small yellow onion, diced

2 garlic cloves, minced

1 tablespoon grated fresh ginger

1½ teaspoons fine sea salt, plus more if needed

1½ teaspoons garam masala

½ teaspoon ground turmeric

½ teaspoon ground coriander

½ teaspoon freshly ground black pepper

⅛ to ¼ teaspoon cayenne pepper, to taste

6 cups cauliflower florets (from 1 small head)

1 cup chopped tomatoes, plus more for garnish

½ cup thawed frozen or cooked fresh green peas

1 tablespoon chopped fresh cilantro, for garnish

Plain yogurt or mashed, salted avocado, for serving (optional)

This aromatic vegetable curry has a zesty sauce enlivened with plenty of tomato, cumin seeds, and ginger. I like it as a main course served over plain rice or Coconut Rice (page 135), but it also makes a complex side dish for a simple roasted chicken or fish. Although not intuitive, sometimes I like to serve this dish with mashed, salted avocado instead of—or in addition to—the yogurt. The avocado adds a rich and dense creaminess that works well with all the spicy vegetables.

---

1. Using the sauté function (set to high, if possible), heat the oil in the pressure cooker pot. Add the cumin seeds and cook until they sizzle and pop, about 1 minute. Add the potatoes and jalapeño and sauté, stirring occasionally, until the jalapeño is softened and the potatoes are light golden in spots, about 6 minutes.

2. Add the onion, garlic, ginger, salt, garam masala, turmeric, coriander, black pepper, and cayenne and sauté until the onion is tender and the spices are fragrant, 3 to 5 minutes.

3. Add the cauliflower, tomatoes, and ⅓ cup water and mix well so everything is coated with the spice mixture.

4. Lock the lid into place and cook on high pressure for 8 minutes. Manually release the pressure.

5. Add the peas to the pot and give the mixture a big stir, breaking up the potatoes and cauliflower a little and incorporating the peas. Cover with the lid (but don't lock it on) and let the curry rest for 5 minutes to warm the peas. Stir again, taste, and add more salt if needed. Garnish with the cilantro and top with yogurt (if using).

CLASSIC TUNA NOODLE CASSEROLE WITH PEAS + DILL

ACTIVE TIME: 20 MINUTES
PRESSURE COOK TIME: 6 MINUTES
TOTAL TIME: 50 TO 55 MINUTES
YIELD: 4 SERVINGS

4 tablespoons (½ stick) unsalted butter, at room temperature

¼ cup chopped onion

1 celery stalk, chopped

2 garlic cloves, thinly sliced

Kosher salt

2¼ cups whole milk, plus more as needed

6 ounces cream cheese, at room temperature

1 teaspoon finely grated lemon zest

½ teaspoon mustard powder

¼ teaspoon freshly ground black pepper

Pinch of cayenne pepper

Pinch of freshly grated nutmeg

8 ounces farfalle (bow-tie pasta)

2 6-ounce cans tuna, drained

1 cup shredded cheddar cheese (4 ounces)

½ cup fresh, cooked peas or frozen green peas, thawed

⅓ cup chopped fresh dill or parsley

A squeeze of lemon juice, to taste

With hits of mustard powder, lemon zest, and garlic, this is more full-flavored than the usual tuna casserole, but just as delectably creamy. If you've got the time and inclination, it's worth taking the extra few minutes to broil the top to make a crispy, cheesy topping—that golden lid of bread crumbs and cheese is irresistible. If you want to go retro, substitute crushed potato chips or Ritz crackers for some or all of the bread crumbs.

1. Using the sauté function, melt 2 tablespoons of the butter in the pressure cooker pot. Stir in the onion, celery, 1 garlic clove, and a pinch of salt and cook until soft, about 5 minutes. Transfer the onion mixture with a slotted spoon to a bowl. Remove the pressure cooker pot from the cooker and set on a heatproof surface to cool.

2. Meanwhile, in a blender, blend the milk, cream cheese, 1 tablespoon of the butter, remaining 1 garlic clove, ¾ teaspoon salt, lemon zest, mustard powder, black pepper, cayenne, and nutmeg until smooth.

3. Brush the remaining 1 tablespoon softened butter over the bottom and a bit up the sides of the cooled pressure cooker pot. Add the cream cheese mixture, onion mixture, and pasta to the pot and stir to combine.

4. Lock the lid into place and cook on high pressure for 6 minutes. Manually release the pressure.

5. Stir the pasta, and if the mixture looks dry, stir in more milk. If the pasta is too al dente for your liking, cover the pot with the lid (but don't lock it on) and let sit for 5 to 10 minutes; the pasta will cook a little more in the residual heat of the pot. When the pasta is done to taste, stir in the tuna, cheddar, peas, dill, and a squeeze of lemon juice. Taste and add more salt and lemon juice if necessary. You can either serve the noodles as they are, or scrape noodles into a gratin dish, cover with crunchy topping, and broil quickly (see below for details)

CRUNCHY TOPPING (OPTIONAL)

1 cup panko bread crumbs

¼ cup grated Parmesan cheese

2 tablespoons unsalted butter, melted

Heat the broiler and place a rack 6 inches from the heat source. In a small bowl, combine the bread crumbs, Parmesan, and melted butter. Scrape the noodles into a shallow gratin dish or 9 x 9-inch baking pan, then top with the bread crumb mixture. Broil until lightly browned on top, 20 seconds to 1½ minutes. Let it cool slightly, then serve.

SPAGHETTI + MEATBALLS

ACTIVE TIME: 25 MINUTES
PRESSURE COOK TIME: 5 MINUTES
TOTAL TIME: 40 MINUTES
YIELD: 4 SERVINGS

FOR THE MEATBALLS

1 pound ground beef

¼ cup panko or regular unseasoned bread crumbs

¼ cup grated Parmesan cheese

1 tablespoon chopped fresh basil

1 large egg

1 teaspoon kosher salt

1 garlic clove, finely grated or minced

FOR THE SAUCE AND PASTA

3 tablespoons extra-virgin olive oil

1 large garlic clove, thinly sliced

¼ teaspoon crushed red pepper flakes

¼ teaspoon freshly ground black pepper

1 28-ounce can crushed tomatoes

2 sprigs fresh basil, plus more thinly sliced for serving

1 teaspoon kosher salt

8 ounces spaghetti (not thin spaghetti), broken in half

2 tablespoons grated Parmesan cheese, plus more (optional) for serving

1 cup ricotta cheese, for serving (optional)

Spaghetti and meatballs isn't necessarily any faster when made in your electric pressure cooker, but it does make things a heck of a lot easier. It can all be done in one pot instead if the usual two or three it would take on the stove. In this version, the meatballs, which are not fried but cooked in the sauce, are full of flavor and very tender—particularly if you use panko bread crumbs, which have a fluffy texture that makes meatballs very light.

I've successfully made this dish using whole wheat spaghetti without changing the recipe at all. But since pasta brands vary a lot, you may have to increase the cooking time if yours turns out too al dente, even after you've let it rest for the full 10 minutes.

Olive fans take note: Adding ¼ cup sliced pitted olives to the sauce as it cooks will probably make you very happy come dinnertime.

1. Make the meatballs: In a large bowl, mix together the beef, panko, Parmesan, basil, egg, salt, and garlic. Roll into 1¼-inch balls.

2. Make the sauce: Using the sauté function, heat 2 tablespoons of the oil in the pressure cooker pot. Stir in the garlic, pepper flakes, and black pepper and cook until fragrant, about 1 minute. Stir in the tomatoes, basil, and salt. Cook, stirring occasionally, for 10 minutes (if the sauce splatters too much, lower the sauté function to low, if possible).

3. Use a fork to remove the basil sprigs from sauce. Scatter the spaghetti over the sauce. Drizzle the remaining 1 tablespoon oil over the spaghetti, stirring gently, then top with the meatballs and 1 cup water.

4. Lock the lid in place and cook on high pressure for 5 minutes. Manually release the pressure.

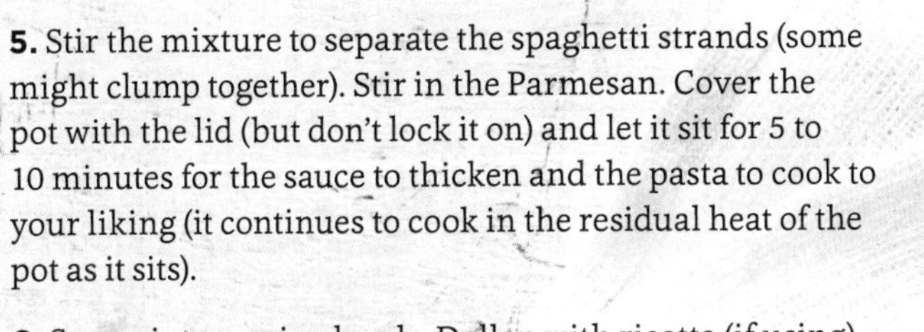

5. Stir the mixture to separate the spaghetti strands (some might clump together). Stir in the Parmesan. Cover the pot with the lid (but don't lock it on) and let it sit for 5 to 10 minutes for the sauce to thicken and the pasta to cook to your liking (it continues to cook in the residual heat of the pot as it sits).

6. Spoon into serving bowls. Dollop with ricotta (if using) and sprinkle with basil and more Parmesan if you like.

CREAMY CHICKPEA PASTA WITH CUMIN + MINT

ACTIVE TIME: 10 MINUTES
PRESSURE COOK TIME: 5 MINUTES
TOTAL TIME: 35 MINUTES
YIELD: 4 SERVINGS

---

6 tablespoons extra-virgin olive oil

1¼ teaspoons cumin seeds

¼ teaspoon crushed red pepper flakes, plus more (optional) for serving

2 garlic cloves, thinly sliced

1 cup (7 ounces) hummus

3¾ cups vegetable broth or chicken stock, preferably homemade (page 109)

16 ounces orecchiette

1 teaspoon kosher salt

1¾ cups cooked chickpeas (from a 14- or 15-ounce can or package)

Fresh lemon juice

½ cup fresh mint leaves, torn

This protein-filled orecchiette dish gets its wonderful thick creaminess from a sauce of hummus mixed with whole chickpeas, while a quickly made cumin-chile oil drizzled in right at the end adds heat, spice, and crunch from the whole cumin seeds. It's an unusual flavor combination for pasta, but with a comforting mac-and-cheese-like texture.

---

1. First, make the cumin oil. Using the sauté function (set to low, if possible), heat 4 tablespoons of the oil in the pressure cooker pot (or you can do this on the stove while the pasta is cooking). Stir in the cumin and pepper flakes and cook until fragrant, about 1 minute. Pour the cumin oil into a small bowl and set aside.

2. Using the sauté function (set to low, if possible), heat the remaining 2 tablespoons oil in the pressure cooker pot. Stir in the garlic and cook until fragrant, about 1 minute. Turn off the sauté function and stir in half of the hummus with a splash of the broth to thin it out, stirring until smooth. Then stir in the remaining broth, the orecchiette, and salt.

3. Lock the lid into place and cook on low pressure for 5 minutes. Manually release the pressure.

4. Stir in the remaining hummus, the chickpeas, lemon juice to taste, and the mint leaves. Drizzle with some of the cumin oil, top with pepper flakes if you like, and serve.

LEMONY SHRIMP + SCALLOP RISOTTO WITH CHIVES

ACTIVE TIME: 10 MINUTES
PRESSURE COOK TIME: 5 MINUTES
TOTAL TIME: 30 MINUTES
YIELD: 4 SERVINGS

---

2 tablespoons extra-virgin olive oil

1½ cups Arborio rice

Fine sea salt

¼ cup dry white wine

3¾ cups vegetable broth or chicken stock, preferably homemade (page 109), or fish stock

Finely grated zest of 1½ lemons

½ pound bay scallops (or sea scallops, quartered), patted dry

½ pound peeled and deveined shrimp, cut into 1-inch pieces

Freshly ground black pepper, to taste

½ cup minced fresh chives

1 tablespoon fresh lemon juice, or more to taste

Freshly grated Parmesan cheese, for serving

This delicately flavored risotto—with lemon, white wine, and a copious amount of minced chives—makes a soft and luscious bed for scallops and shrimp. In order to keep the seafood tender and succulent, instead of cooking it under pressure, I add it after the risotto is finished, and let the residual heat of the pot cook the bite-size pieces of shellfish; this only takes a few minutes. You can use any kind of mild stock here, preferably homemade. I like vegetable broth because it has the gentlest flavor, but fish or chicken stock also work well.

---

1. Using the sauté function, heat the oil in the pressure cooker pot. Stir in the rice and 1¼ teaspoons salt and cook until the rice is lightly toasted, 3 to 5 minutes. Stir in the wine and cook until it has evaporated, about 1 minute. Stir in the broth and about two-thirds of the lemon zest.

2. Lock the lid into place and cook on high pressure for 5 minutes. Manually release the pressure.

3. Meanwhile, season the scallops and shrimp lightly with salt and pepper.

4. Once the pressure is released, stir the risotto for a few times so the rice absorbs some of the excess liquid. Then, working quickly so the rice stays hot, fold in the seafood, remaining lemon zest, pepper to taste, chives, and lemon juice. Cover the pot with the lid (but don't lock it on) and let it sit for 3 to 5 minutes, until the seafood is cooked through. To serve, spoon into bowls and sprinkle with Parmesan.

BARLEY RISOTTO WITH PROSCIUTTO, GOAT CHEESE + RADICCHIO

ACTIVE TIME: 20 MINUTES
PRESSURE COOK TIME: 22 MINUTES
TOTAL TIME: 55 MINUTES
YIELD: 4 SERVINGS

---

2 tablespoons extra-virgin olive oil, plus more for drizzling

2 ounces prosciutto, diced or coarsely chopped

2 leeks (white and light green parts only), halved and thinly sliced (or use 1 Spanish onion)

1½ cups pearl barley

1 garlic clove, finely grated or minced

1 teaspoon kosher salt, plus more if needed

¼ cup dry white wine

3¾ cups chicken stock or vegetable broth, preferably homemade (page 108)

1 cup thinly sliced radicchio

¼ cup packed fresh parsley leaves

Fresh lemon juice

⅓ cup grated Parmesan cheese

2 ounces fresh goat cheese, crumbled, at room temperature

¼ teaspoon freshly ground black pepper, plus more if needed

Barley makes for a slightly chewier and more substantial risotto than the usual rice, with a nutty flavor. This one is creamy from the goat cheese and Parmesan, with a salty, porky flavor from bits of sautéed prosciutto. Topped with a crisp and colorful radicchio and parsley salad, this dish is bright and multitextured. If you'd rather make this vegetarian, leave out the prosciutto and use vegetable broth. It's just as good without the meat, though you might want to increase the Parmesan to make up for the missing salt.

---

1. Using the sauté function, heat 1 tablespoon of the oil in the pressure cooker pot. Stir in the prosciutto and cook until the pieces are golden at the edges, 2 to 4 minutes. Transfer the prosciutto with a slotted spoon to a plate lined with paper towels.

2. Add the remaining 1 tablespoon oil to the pot and stir in the leeks. Cook until the leeks are tender, 3 to 5 minutes. Stir in the barley, garlic, and salt. Cook, stirring frequently, until the barley is starting to brown, 2 to 4 minutes. Stir the wine into the pot until it has been absorbed, about 1 minute. Stir in the stock.

3. Lock the lid into place and cook on high pressure for 22 minutes. Let the pressure release naturally for 10 minutes, then manually release the remaining pressure.

4. Meanwhile, in a medium bowl, toss together the radicchio and parsley with a squeeze of lemon juice, a drizzle of olive oil, and a pinch of salt.

5. Stir the reserved prosciutto, Parmesan, goat cheese, and pepper into the risotto. Cover the pot with the lid (but don't lock it on) and let the risotto sit for 5 minutes to finish cooking. Taste and add more salt and pepper if necessary. Serve topped with the radicchio mixture, which will wilt a little when it hits the hot risotto. Squeeze on a little more lemon juice right at the end, if you like.

PESTO RISOTTO
WITH CHERRY TOMATOES + MOZZARELLA

ACTIVE TIME: 15 MINUTES
PRESSURE COOK TIME: 5 MINUTES
TOTAL TIME: 30 MINUTES
YIELD: 4 SERVINGS

FOR THE RISOTTO

2 tablespoons extra-virgin olive oil

1½ cups Arborio rice

1½ teaspoons kosher salt

¼ cup dry white wine

2 cups cherry tomatoes, halved if large

About 3 cups vegetable broth, preferably homemade (page 109)

FOR THE PESTO

2 tablespoons pine nuts or slivered almonds

¼ cup grated Parmesan cheese

¼ cup extra-virgin olive oil

1½ ounces fresh basil, leaves and tender stems (about 1½ cups)

1 garlic clove, finely grated

Large pinch of kosher salt

---

8 ounces mozzarella, cut into bite-size pieces

Freshly grated Parmesan cheese, for serving

This creamy, herbal vegetarian risotto has a combination of condensed, cooked cherry tomatoes and juicy raw ones, which contribute both a depth of flavor and freshness. To this I add chunks of mozzarella that partially melt in the rice's heat, and a swirl of homemade, garlicky pesto, which makes it rich and pungent. If you're short on time, you can substitute prepared pesto for the homemade.

---

1. Make the risotto: Using the sauté function, heat the oil in the pressure cooker pot. Stir in the rice and salt and cook until the rice is lightly toasted, 3 to 5 minutes. Stir in the wine and cook until it has evaporated, about 1 minute.

2. Pour half of the cherry tomatoes into a 4-cup measuring cup. Pour enough broth over the tomatoes to reach 3½ cups. Stir the mixture into the rice.

3. Lock the lid into place and cook on high pressure for 5 minutes. Manually release the pressure.

4. While the risotto cooks, make the pesto: Heat a small skillet over medium heat. Stir in the nuts and cook until lightly toasted, about 3 minutes. Scrape into a mini food processor or blender. Add the Parmesan, oil, basil, garlic, and salt. Blend until smooth.

5. Once the pressure has released, stir the risotto until it turns creamy and the liquid has been absorbed, 3 to 5 minutes. Fold in the pesto, the remaining tomatoes, and the mozzarella. To serve, spoon the risotto into bowls and sprinkle with Parmesan.

RISOTTO CARBONARA

ACTIVE TIME: 15 MINUTES
PRESSURE COOK TIME: 6 MINUTES
TOTAL TIME: 45 MINUTES
YIELD: 4 SERVINGS

---

1 tablespoon extra-virgin olive oil

3 ounces pancetta or slab bacon, cubed

1 garlic clove, finely grated or minced

1½ cups Arborio rice

1 teaspoon kosher salt

¼ cup dry white wine

3¾ cups chicken stock, preferably homemade (page 108)

2 large egg yolks

½ cup grated Pecorino Romano cheese (about 2 ounces)

1 teaspoon freshly ground black pepper

Elegant enough to serve to company but fast enough for any given weeknight, this wonderfully rich risotto gets a brawny character from the pancetta, along with a pleasingly sharp kick from the Pecorino Romano cheese. If you want to add a bit of color, stir in ½ cup thawed frozen peas right at the end.

---

1. Using the sauté function, heat the oil in the pressure cooker pot. Stir in the pancetta and cook until the fat is rendered and the pancetta is crisp, about 5 minutes. Transfer with a slotted spoon to a plate lined with paper towels and set aside. Leave fat in pot.

2. Stir the garlic into the pot and cook until fragrant, about 30 seconds. Stir in the rice and salt and cook, stirring frequently, until the rice starts to turn golden, 2 to 4 minutes.

3. Stir the wine into the pot and cook, stirring, until it has been absorbed, about 1 minute. Stir in the stock.

4. Lock the lid into place and cook on high pressure for 6 minutes. Manually release the pressure.

5. In a medium bowl, whisk together the egg yolks, Pecorino Romano, and black pepper until smooth. Stir into the risotto (the heat of the rice will cook the egg). Add the reserved pancetta. Taste, adjust the seasonings if necessary, and serve.

RED LENTIL DAL
WITH COCONUT

ACTIVE TIME: 20 MINUTES
PRESSURE COOK TIME: 6 MINUTES
TOTAL TIME: 50 MINUTES
YIELD: 4 SERVINGS

3 tablespoons unsalted butter

1 teaspoon cumin seeds

1 teaspoon coriander seeds

1 small red onion, thinly sliced

½-inch piece fresh ginger, peeled and finely grated or chopped (about 1 teaspoon)

2 garlic cloves, finely grated or minced

½ teaspoon cracked black pepper

½ teaspoon ground turmeric

½ teaspoon chili powder

1½ cups red lentils

1½ teaspoons kosher salt

1 14.5-ounce can diced tomatoes

Cooked rice, for serving

Coconut cream or full-fat coconut milk, for serving (or use yogurt)

Chopped cilantro or mint, for garnish

Dal is a classic Indian dish of soft-cooked and spiced lentils, peas, or beans, usually served with rice. This simple, fragrant everyday version gets a mild sweetness from the coconut cream stirred in at the end. But if you'd rather go in a tangier direction, you can substitute plain yogurt.

1. Using the sauté function, melt the butter in the pressure cooker pot. Add the cumin and coriander seeds and toast until fragrant, about 1 minute. Add the onion and cook, tossing occasionally, until pale golden brown and tender, 2 to 3 minutes. Add the ginger, garlic, black pepper, turmeric, and chili powder and sauté for 1 minute.

2. Add the lentils, 3½ cups water, and the salt. Lock the lid into place and cook on high pressure for 6 minutes. Let the pressure release naturally for 10 minutes, then manually release the remaining pressure.

3. Taste for seasoning, adding more salt if needed. Pour the tomatoes and juices into the pot. Using the sauté function, simmer the liquid on low for 2 minutes to meld the flavors. (If the dal begins to sputter, turn off the sauté function and let the pot sit for another minute or two.)

4. Spoon the dal over bowls of rice. Serve plain or topped with coconut cream and cilantro.

COOK IT SLOW

Cook on high for 2 to 3 hours or low for 5 to 6 hours. Add the tomatoes and juice in the last 15 minutes of cooking.

FAST WEEKNIGHT COMFORT

CHICKEN, MEAT + SEAFOOD

CHICKEN CACCIATORE WITH MUSHROOMS

ACTIVE TIME: 25 MINUTES
PRESSURE COOK TIME: 13 MINUTES
TOTAL TIME: 55 MINUTES
YIELD: 3 TO 4 SERVINGS

2 tablespoons extra-virgin olive oil, plus more as needed

2 pounds bone-in, skin-on chicken thighs, patted dry

Kosher salt and freshly ground black pepper

4 ounces cremini or white button mushrooms, thinly sliced

1 small yellow onion, thinly sliced

1 small red bell pepper, thinly sliced

2 garlic cloves, thinly sliced

¾ cup canned diced tomatoes and their liquid

¼ cup dry white or red wine (or use more of the canned, diced tomato)

2 large sprigs rosemary

2 tablespoons drained capers

Chopped fresh basil or parsley, for garnish (optional)

COOK IT SLOW

After browning the chicken and vegetables, return the chicken to the pot and add the tomatoes, wine, and rosemary. Slow cook on high for 3 to 4 hours or low for 4 to 5 hours.

In this Italian classic, bone-in chicken is quickly braised in a tomato and mushroom sauce spiked with bell pepper and garlic. Sometimes I slip a few minced anchovies into the pot along with the vegetables for an extra savory, salty oompf. This is excellent served over egg noodles, orzo, or polenta.

1. Using the sauté function (set on high, if possible), heat 1 tablespoon of the oil in the pressure cooker pot. Season the chicken with 1 teaspoon salt and ¼ teaspoon pepper and arrange the thighs in a single layer, skin-side down, on the bottom of the pot. (Work in batches if they don't fit in a single layer, adding more oil for each batch.) Cook, without moving, until well browned, about 8 minutes. Transfer the chicken to a plate as it browns. (You only have to brown it on one side.)

2. Add the remaining 1 tablespoon oil to the pot along with the mushrooms, onion, bell pepper, garlic, and a pinch of salt. Sauté until the vegetables are tender and golden, about 5 minutes.

3. Add the tomatoes, wine, and rosemary and bring to a simmer, using a wooden spoon to scrape up any browned bits on the bottom of the pot. Let simmer for 1 minute to cook off some of the alcohol from the wine. Place the chicken, browned side up, in the pot and pour in any accumulated juices.

4. Lock the lid into place and cook on high pressure for 13 minutes. Let the pressure release naturally for 10 minutes, then manually release the remaining pressure.

5. Transfer the chicken to serving plates; keep loosely tented with foil. Add the capers to the pot. Using the sauté function, bring the sauce to a simmer and cook until thickened slightly, 5 to 7 minutes. Taste and adjust the seasoning if necessary. Remove the rosemary stems. Spoon the sauce over the chicken and top with chopped basil or parsley, if desired.

WEEKNIGHT CHICKEN PARMESAN

ACTIVE TIME: 15 MINUTES
PRESSURE COOK TIME: 3 MINUTES
TOTAL TIME: 20 MINUTES
YIELD: 2 TO 3 SERVINGS

---

1 tablespoon extra-virgin olive oil

2 garlic cloves, thinly sliced

1½ cups prepared marinara sauce (or use the sauce from Spaghetti + Meatballs, page 46)

3 tablespoons grated Parmesan cheese

Freshly ground black pepper

4 thin chicken cutlets (10 to 12 ounces total)

½ teaspoon kosher salt, or more to taste

½ teaspoon dried oregano

4 ounces fresh mozzarella cheese, grated

Chopped basil, for garnish (optional)

No frying, no breading, this easy, Chicken Parm–inspired dish is lean and weeknight fast. Broiling the cheese after cooking is an added step worth doing if you've got the extra few minutes to spare—it makes everything golden brown and a little crisp at the edges. If you have leftover marinara sauce, either freeze it or toss with some pasta to serve on the side.

For more flavor here, add a few tablespoons of chopped olives, anchovies, or capers to the pot along with the sauce.

---

1. Using the sauté function (on low, if possible), heat the oil in the pressure cooker pot. Stir in the garlic and cook until just turning golden, 2 to 4 minutes. Stir in the marinara sauce, 2 tablespoons of the Parmesan, and ¼ teaspoon pepper. Increase the sauté heat to medium.

2. Season the chicken with the salt, oregano, and pepper to taste. Nestle the cutlets into the sauce, overlapping as little as possible, then spoon the sauce over to cover the chicken.

3. Lock the lid into place and cook on low pressure for 3 minutes. Manually release the pressure.

4. Sprinkle the mozzarella and the remaining 1 tablespoon Parmesan evenly over the chicken. Cover the pot with the lid (but don't lock it on) and let it sit for 4 to 5 minutes to melt the cheese. Serve as is or, for deeper flavors and a little bit of crispiness, broil the cheese until golden and bubbling: Heat the broiler with a rack 4 inches from the heat source. Scoop the chicken and sauce into a greased small rimmed baking sheet, trying to keep the cheese on top. Broil until the cheese has browned, 2 to 3 minutes. Sprinkle with basil, if desired.

CHICKEN WITH MARINATED ARTICHOKES, SHALLOTS + BASIL

ACTIVE TIME: 20 MINUTES
PRESSURE COOK TIME: 12 MINUTES
TOTAL TIME: 40 MINUTES
YIELD: 2 TO 3 SERVINGS

---

2 tablespoons extra-virgin olive oil, plus more as needed

6 garlic cloves, peeled

1 shallot, quartered

1¼ pounds bone-in, skin-on chicken thighs, patted dry

¾ teaspoon kosher salt

¼ teaspoon freshly ground black pepper

1½ cups (from about a 12-ounce jar) marinated artichoke hearts, drained and rinsed

½ tablespoon fresh lemon juice

2 tablespoons white wine

Sliced fresh basil, for serving

Lemon wedges, for serving

COOK IT SLOW

After step 3, slow cook on high for 3 to 4 hours or low for 4 to 5 hours.

A jar of good-quality marinated artichoke hearts is the kind of pantry staple that can do a lot to gussy up your average weeknight chicken. Here, the artichokes and chicken share the pot with browned shallots and whole garlic cloves, which add sweetness and depth. Use the best marinated artichoke hearts you can get; it makes all the difference. Some larger supermarkets even sell them out of bins in bulk (along with the olives), and those will usually have the finest flavor and texture.

---

1. Using the sauté function (set on high, if possible), heat the oil in the pressure cooker pot. Add the whole garlic cloves and shallot quarters and sauté until golden in spots, 3 to 4 minutes. Use a slotted spoon to transfer the vegetables to a small bowl or plate.

2. Season both sides of the chicken thighs with the salt and pepper. Arrange them in a single layer, skin-side down, on the bottom of the pot. If the pot looks dry, add a little more oil before adding the chicken. (If the chicken doesn't fit in a single layer, cook in batches, adding more oil as needed.) Cook until browned on one side, about 5 minutes, then flip the chicken over. (You don't have to brown it on the other side.)

3. When all the chicken is browned, return it to the pot if you've taken it out. Scatter the garlic, shallot, and artichoke hearts over the chicken. Drizzle with the lemon juice and white wine.

4. Lock the lid into place and cook on high pressure for 12 minutes. Manually release the pressure.

5. Transfer the chicken and artichokes to serving plates. Using the sauté function, simmer the sauce remaining in the pot, cooking for about 3 minutes to reduce and thicken. Spoon the sauce over the chicken and artichokes, sprinkle with basil, and serve with lemon wedges on the side.

CUBAN CHICKEN + RICE

ACTIVE TIME: 25 MINUTES
PRESSURE COOK TIME: 5 MINUTES
TOTAL TIME: 50 MINUTES
YIELD: 4 SERVINGS

---

2 tablespoons fresh orange juice

2 tablespoons fresh lime juice

3 garlic cloves, finely grated or minced

1¾ teaspoons kosher salt, plus more as needed

¾ teaspoon ground cumin

½ teaspoon dried oregano

¼ teaspoon cayenne pepper

¼ teaspoon ground coriander

1¾ to 2 pounds boneless, skinless chicken thighs

3 tablespoons extra-virgin olive oil

1 red onion, diced

½ cup diced green bell pepper

1 serrano or jalapeño chile, seeded and diced

1 tablespoon tomato paste

1¼ cups long-grain white rice

¾ cup chicken stock, preferably homemade (page 108), or water

⅔ cup sliced green olives with pimientos (or other pitted olives)

Chopped parsley, for serving

Based on a classic arroz con pollo, this weeknight chicken and rice dish doesn't stint on the garlicky, citrusy, peppery flavors of the original version, but gets you there much more quickly. Don't substitute boneless chicken breasts for the thighs here: They will dry out in the time it takes for the rice to cook. Bone-in breasts will work a lot better, though they still won't be as tender as the thighs—which, after marinating and pressure-cooking, turn positively silky.

---

1. In a large bowl, combine the orange juice, lime juice, garlic, 1½ teaspoons of the salt, the cumin, oregano, cayenne, and coriander. Add the chicken thighs, tossing to coat. Let marinate for at least 10 minutes at room temperature, and up to overnight in the fridge.

2. Meanwhile, using the sauté function (on high if possible), heat the oil in the pressure cooker pot. Stir in the onion, bell pepper, chile, and ¼ teaspoon salt. Cook until starting to brown, 6 to 10 minutes. Stir in the tomato paste and cook for another 1 minute. Turn off the sauté function.

3. Stir in the rice until it's coated in oil, then stir in the stock. Lay the chicken and all the marinade from the bowl over the rice in an even layer.

4. Lock the lid into place and cook on high pressure for 5 minutes. Manually release the pressure.

5. Fold the rice and chicken together (the chicken will naturally break up into large chunks as you do this). Taste it and add more salt if needed, and, if the rice is a little too al dente, cover the pot with the lid (don't lock it on) and let it sit for 5 minutes. Stir in the olives and serve topped with parsley.

LEMON CHICKEN WITH GARLIC + OLIVES

ACTIVE TIME: 20 MINUTES
PRESSURE COOK TIME: 15 MINUTES
TOTAL TIME: 45 MINUTES
YIELD: 3 TO 4 SERVINGS

---

1 tablespoon extra-virgin olive oil, plus more as needed

2 pounds bone-in, skin-on chicken thighs, patted dry (4 to 6, depending on the size)

¾ teaspoon kosher salt, plus more if needed

¼ teaspoon freshly ground black pepper

½ cup chicken stock, preferably homemade (page 108)

⅓ cup mixed pitted olives

4 thin slices lemon

4 garlic cloves, thinly sliced

2 anchovy fillets, chopped (optional)

1 tablespoon drained capers

1 teaspoon fresh rosemary needles, chopped

1 teaspoon fresh thyme leaves, chopped, plus more for garnish

½ teaspoon fennel seeds, lightly crushed with a mortar and pestle or with the flat side of a knife

---

Heady with garlic, lemon, olives, and plenty of herbs, these braised, bone-in chicken thighs are spoonably succulent and surrounded by a deeply flavorful, rich sauce. I love this dish served over a mound of polenta, but mashed potatoes or egg noodles are also excellent for soaking up the sauce.

---

1. Using the sauté function (set on high if possible), heat the oil in the pressure cooker pot. Season the chicken with the salt and pepper and arrange in a single layer, skin-side down, on the bottom of the pot. (Work in batches if they don't fit in a single layer, adding more oil for each batch.) Cook, without moving, until well browned, about 8 minutes. (You only have to brown it on one side).

2. Flip the chicken, pour in the stock, and scatter with the olives, lemon slices, garlic, anchovies (if using), capers, rosemary, thyme, and fennel seeds.

3. Lock the lid into place and cook on high pressure for 15 minutes. Let the pressure naturally release.

4. Discard the lemon slices and transfer the chicken to serving plates; keep loosely tented with foil. Using the sauté function, bring the sauce to a simmer and cook until thickened slightly, 3 to 5 minutes. Taste and adjust the salt and pepper if necessary. Spoon the sauce over the chicken and serve garnished with thyme.

COOK IT SLOW

After step 2, slow cook on high for 3 to 4 hours or low for 4 to 5 hours.

SIMPLE POACHED CHICKEN BREASTS + THREE SAUCES

ACTIVE TIME: 5 MINUTES
PRESSURE COOK TIME: 5 MINUTES
TOTAL TIME: 25 MINUTES
YIELD: 2 TO 4 SERVINGS

---

1 quart chicken stock, preferably homemade (page 108)

Salt

2 large boneless, skinless chicken breasts (about 8 ounces each)

Sauce of choice (recipes follow)

It can be hard to cook chicken breasts perfectly in your pressure cooker; they tend to go from juicy to desiccated in seconds. But when covered in chicken stock and cooked on low pressure for a few minutes, they come out just right—moist, tender, and very flavorful. After cooking, don't discard the liquid in the pot. Freeze it and use the intense, double-strength broth whenever you need a good, strong stock—it's excellent for sauces, stews, and soups.

Serve the poached chicken breasts topped with one of the three sauces: The soy and sesame sauce is creamy and spicy, the jalapeño green sauce is herbal and tangy, and the honey-mustard aioli is both sweet and sharp. Or, just poach the chicken to have on hand to shred on top of salads or slice into sandwiches.

---

1. Pour the stock into the pressure cooker pot and season generously with salt (this is especially important if your stock is unsalted). Add the chicken breasts to the pot.

2. Lock the lid into place and cook on low pressure for 5 minutes. Manually release the pressure.

3. Remove the chicken from the stock, cut a slit in the center of each breast, and check to make sure it is cooked all the way through. If not, put one or both breasts back in the broth, cover the pot with the lid (don't lock it on), and let the chicken finish cooking in the residual heat of the pot.

4. Serve with one of the sauces or, if not using the chicken immediately, let the chicken cool and then store in its broth in the refrigerator for up to 3 days.

SOY + SESAME SAUCE

⅓ cup sugar

¼ cup soy sauce

¼ cup Chinkiang (Chinese black) vinegar or balsamic vinegar

2 teaspoons toasted sesame oil

⅓ cup hot chili oil

¼ cup tahini

½ teaspoon freshly ground Sichuan peppercorns or black pepper

½ cup thinly sliced scallions, for serving

½ cup cilantro leaves, for serving

Chopped roasted peanuts, for serving

1. In a small pot (or use the sauté function of your pressure cooker), combine the sugar and soy sauce. Cook over medium heat until the sugar dissolves.

2. Remove from the heat and transfer to a bowl. Whisk in the vinegar, sesame oil, chili oil, tahini, and pepper. To serve, top sliced chicken with sauce, scallions, cilantro, and peanuts.

JALAPEÑO GREEN SAUCE

1½ cups fresh cilantro leaves and tender stems

3 to 4 jalapeño chiles, seeded and diced

2 garlic cloves, finely grated or minced

¼ cup grated Parmesan cheese, plus more for serving

2 tablespoons fresh lime juice, plus more if needed

1 teaspoon kosher salt, plus more if needed

½ teaspoon ancho chile powder

¾ cup extra-virgin olive oil, plus more for drizzling

1. In a food processor or blender, puree the cilantro, jalapeños, garlic, Parmesan, lime juice, salt, and ancho powder. With the motor running, drizzle in the oil until the sauce is emulsified. Taste and add more salt or lime juice if needed.

2. Serve the sauce over the sliced chicken. Garnish with some Parmesan and a drizzle of olive oil.

HONEY-MUSTARD AIOLI

1 teaspoon plus 3 tablespoons Dijon mustard

1 tablespoon fresh lemon juice, plus more if needed

1 large egg yolk

¼ teaspoon fine sea salt, plus more if needed

¾ cup neutral oil, such as safflower or canola

2 tablespoons honey

1 tablespoon whole-grain mustard

1. In a medium bowl or blender, whisk or blend to combine 1 teaspoon of the Dijon mustard, the lemon juice, egg yolk, and salt. Whisking constantly, or with the blender on low, slowly drizzle in the oil. Once the mixture is thick and emulsified, you can drizzle the oil in more quickly.

2. Fold in the remaining 3 tablespoons Dijon mustard, the honey, and whole-grain mustard. Taste and add more salt and lemon juice if needed.

3. Slice the chicken and serve with dollops of the sauce on the side.

CHICKEN WITH PEANUT SAUCE

ACTIVE TIME: 15 MINUTES
PRESSURE COOK TIME: 8 MINUTES
TOTAL TIME: 35 MINUTES
YIELD: 3 TO 4 SERVINGS

¼ cup creamy peanut butter

2 tablespoons soy sauce, or more to taste

1½ tablespoons light brown sugar, or more to taste

1 tablespoon chopped fresh cilantro

1 tablespoon finely grated fresh ginger

½ tablespoon fresh lime juice, or more to taste

1 garlic clove, finely grated or minced

1-inch piece lemongrass stalk (optional), chopped

¼ teaspoon crushed red pepper flakes, or more to taste

½ cup chicken stock, preferably homemade (page 108), or water

1¼ pounds boneless, skinless chicken thighs

Sliced scallions, for serving

Chopped peanuts, for serving

COOK IT SLOW

Cook on high for 3 to 4 hours or low for 4 to 5 hours.

This has all the alluring peanut-chile-lemongrass flavors of Thai chicken satay, except that the meat is cooked under pressure until exceptionally tender instead of being grilled. It's faster than takeout, and just as crave-worthy. If you want to use white meat instead of thighs, substitute boneless, skinless breasts and reduce the cooking time to 5 minutes, then let the pressure release naturally for 5 minutes before manually releasing the remaining pressure.

Serve this over Coconut Rice (page 135) for a gently sweet side dish.

---

1. In a blender, combine 3 tablespoons water, the peanut butter, 1 tablespoon of the soy sauce, ½ tablespoon of the brown sugar, the cilantro, ½ tablespoon of the ginger, the lime juice, garlic, lemongrass (if using), and red pepper flakes. Blend until smooth, adding a little more water if needed; you're looking for a thick, mayonnaise-like texture. Taste and add more lime juice, sugar, red pepper flakes, or soy sauce if you like. Scrape the sauce into a small bowl. Set the peanut sauce aside.

2. Pour the chicken stock into the pressure cooker pot, then stir in the remaining 1 tablespoon soy sauce, 1 tablespoon brown sugar, and ½ tablespoon ginger. Add the chicken thighs to the pot, turning to coat them in the liquid.

3. Lock the lid into place and cook on high pressure for 8 minutes. Let the pressure release naturally for 5 minutes, then manually release the remaining pressure.

4. Transfer the chicken to serving plates (discard the cooking liquid). Top with the scallions and peanuts, and serve with the peanut sauce on the side.

CHIPOTLE BROWN SUGAR SALMON

ACTIVE TIME: 15 MINUTES
PRESSURE COOK TIME: 1 MINUTE
TOTAL TIME: 25 MINUTES
YIELD: 3 SERVINGS

Finely grated zest and juice of 2 small oranges or 2 large tangerines

Finely grated zest and juice of 2 limes

2½ tablespoons brown sugar

2 tablespoons soy sauce

1½ teaspoons chopped chipotle chile in adobo sauce

1 garlic clove, finely grated or minced

3 salmon fillets (6 to 8 ounces each), preferably center-cut

Sliced scallions, for serving

Using the low pressure setting cooks salmon gently, without drying it out. Here, I flavor the pink fillets with orange, lime, chipotle chiles, and some brown sugar to help caramelize the top. It's a little spicy, a little sweet, and very bright from the citrus.

---

1. Using the sauté function, whisk together the orange zest, orange juice, lime zest, lime juice, brown sugar, soy sauce, chipotle, and garlic in the pressure cooker pot. Bring to a simmer and then turn off the sauté function. Taste and adjust the seasoning if necessary, adding more sugar or soy sauce if it's too sour or needs more salt.

2. Place the fish in the sauce in the pressure cooker (skin-side up, if it's still attached). Spoon the sauce over the fish so it is completely covered.

3. Lock the lid into place and cook on low pressure for 1 minute. Let the pressure release naturally for 5 minutes, then manually release the remaining pressure.

4. Check the fish for doneness by cutting into one of the fillets; it should be lighter pink at the top and darker pink in the center. If you prefer your salmon more well done, cook it for another minute using the sauté function.

5. Carefully lift the salmon fillets onto a serving platter, flipping them over so the browned sides are facing up.

6. Using the sauté function, reduce the sauce in the pressure cooker pot until it is thick and syrupy, about 2 minutes. Spoon the sauce over the salmon and garnish with scallions.

EASY WEEKNIGHT CHILI

ACTIVE TIME: 25 MINUTES
PRESSURE COOK TIME: 8 MINUTES
TOTAL TIME: 55 MINUTES
YIELD: 3 TO 4 SERVINGS

2 tablespoons extra-virgin olive oil
1 pound ground pork or beef
2 teaspoons kosher salt, more to taste
1 large onion, diced
1 green bell pepper, diced
1 serrano or jalapeño chile, seeded (if desired) and diced
4 garlic cloves, finely grated or minced
1 tablespoon tomato paste
2 tablespoons chili powder
1 teaspoon dried oregano
½ teaspoon ground cumin
1 14.5-ounce can diced tomatoes
2 15-ounce cans pinto or kidney beans, drained and rinsed
½ cup chopped fresh cilantro leaves and tender stems
Fresh lime juice
Sour cream, for serving
Cubed avocado, for serving (optional)

COOK IT SLOW

After step 3, slow cook on high for 2 to 3 hours or low for 4 to 5 hours.

Pork gives this relatively fast chili a full, rich flavor, but you can also use beef here, as long as it's not too lean: 80% is about right. This chili is relatively mild, so if you're looking for something more intense, consider adding a big pinch of cayenne or an extra serrano chile or two. Chili freezes perfectly, so feel free to double this recipe. Just be sure to sear the meat in two batches; otherwise you could end up steaming instead of browning it. Serve as is, over rice, or as a taco filling with the avocado and sour cream.

1. Using the sauté function (set on high, if possible), heat 1 tablespoon of the oil in the pressure cooker pot. Add half the meat, spread it over the oil, and let it brown without stirring (this helps encourage browning) for 5 to 7 minutes. Give the meat a good stir and sauté for 1 more minute. Use a slotted spoon to transfer the meat to a plate and season with ½ teaspoon of the salt. Repeat with the remaining 1 tablespoon oil, meat, and another ½ teaspoon salt.

2. Stir the onion, bell pepper, diced chile, garlic, and ½ teaspoon of the salt into the pot and cook until softened, about 5 minutes.

3. Stir in the tomato paste, chili powder, oregano, and cumin and cook until fragrant, about 1 minute. Stir in the meat and any juices from the plate, along with the tomatoes, beans, and remaining ½ teaspoon salt.

4. Lock the lid into place and cook on high pressure for 8 minutes. Let the pressure release naturally.

5. Stir in the cilantro and a squeeze or two of lime juice, then taste and adjust the lime juice and salt if necessary. Serve with the sour cream and avocado (if using).

CHICKEN ADOBO WITH SOY SAUCE + GINGER

ACTIVE TIME: 20 MINUTES
PRESSURE COOK TIME: 15 MINUTES
TOTAL TIME: 55 MINUTES
YIELD: 4 TO 6 SERVINGS

½ cup cane vinegar, malt vinegar, or apple cider vinegar

½ cup soy sauce

2 teaspoons palm sugar or dark brown sugar

½ teaspoon freshly ground black pepper

1 small head garlic (about 10 cloves), coarsely chopped

1-inch piece fresh ginger, peeled and cut into matchsticks

2 bay leaves

1 to 2 fresh green Thai chiles (or serrano or jalapeño), halved lengthwise

2½ pounds bone-in, skin-on chicken thighs and drumsticks

1 tablespoon neutral oil, such as sunflower or grapeseed, plus more as needed

Cilantro leaves, for garnish (optional)

Coconut Rice (page 135), for serving

Cooked in a mixture of soy sauce, ginger, chiles, and an entire head of garlic, Philippine adobo chicken is one of the more intensely flavored poultry dishes out there. There are myriad versions of the dish, some with coconut milk mixed into the sauce, and some, like this one, served with coconut rice on the side. Cane vinegar, made from fermented sugar cane juice, adds a molasses-like richness here, but malt or cider vinegar can be substituted.

This recipe comes from our family friend John Mendiola, who learned it from his mother, Carmelita, a passionate cook originally from Manila.

---

1. In a large bowl, combine the vinegar, soy sauce, sugar, black pepper, garlic, ginger, bay leaves, and chiles. Add the chicken and let it marinate for at least 10 minutes or, even better, overnight in the refrigerator.

2. Using the sauté function (set on high, if possible), heat the oil in the pressure cooker pot. Remove the chicken from the marinade and pat dry (reserve the marinade).

3. Arrange the chicken in a single layer on the bottom of the pot. (Work in batches if the pieces don't fit in a single layer, adding more oil for each batch.) Cook until well browned, 2 to 4 minutes per side, transferring the pieces to a plate as they brown. Add the marinade to the pot, scraping up the browned bits on the bottom of the pot. Return the chicken and any accumulated juices to the pot.

4. Lock the lid into place and cook on high pressure for 15 minutes. Let the pressure release naturally.

5. Transfer the chicken to a serving platter and tent with foil to keep warm. Remove the bay leaves from the sauce. Using the sauté function (on high, if possible), simmer the sauce until it's thick and has the consistency of a glaze, 10 to 15 minutes.

6. Spoon the glaze over the chicken and serve with coconut rice. Garnish with cilantro leaves, if you like.

COOK IT SLOW

After step 3, slow cook on high for 3 to 4 hours or low for 4 to 5. Proceed with step 5. If the sauce is not thickened to your liking, continue cooking on high to reduce for another 15 to 30 minutes.

SRIRACHA TURKEY MEATLOAF WITH BUTTERED POTATOES

ACTIVE TIME: 15 MINUTES
PRESSURE COOK TIME: 35 MINUTES
TOTAL TIME: 55 MINUTES
YIELD: 3 TO 4 SERVINGS

Olive oil, for greasing the pan

2 medium russet (baking) potatoes (1¼ pounds total), quartered lengthwise into spears

Kosher salt

1 pound ground turkey, preferably not white meat

1 small yellow onion, finely diced

¾ cup panko bread crumbs

2 large eggs

¼ cup finely chopped fresh cilantro or parsley, plus more for the potatoes

1½ tablespoons Sriracha (or another hot sauce), plus more for serving

2 garlic cloves, finely grated or minced

1 teaspoon dried oregano

¼ teaspoon ground cumin

2 tablespoons ketchup

Butter, for serving

Meatloaf and buttered potatoes is pretty much the ultimate in comfort-food meals, one that conjures 1950s images of familial coziness. This version keeps the cozy factor but gets a kick from the Sriracha and a little cumin mixed into the meat. I like the spicy sweetness of Sriracha here, but any hot sauce can be substituted. Note that if you'd rather make this with ground beef instead of turkey, you absolutely can.

If you don't have a 7-inch springform pan, you can form the meatloaf mixture into a 7-inch round and wrap it in two layers of foil instead.

---

1. Brush a 7-inch springform pan (or two layers of aluminum foil) with olive oil. Pour 1½ cups water into the pressure cooker pot. Place a steamer rack/trivet in the bottom.

2. Poke the potato spears all over with a fork and sprinkle them with salt. Make two foil packets of 4 potato spears each, with the spears lying next to each other, not on top of one another (so the package will lie flat). Stack both packets on top of one another on the steamer rack (keeping the potato packets flat is essential or the meatloaf pan may not fit on top with enough room to lock on the lid).

3. In a large bowl, combine the turkey, onion, panko, egg, cilantro, ½ tablespoon of the Sriracha, the garlic, 1 teaspoon salt, the oregano, and cumin. Press evenly into the prepared springform pan (or wrap in the foil). Cover the pan tightly with aluminum foil. Place the meatloaf pan directly on top of the potato packets.

4. Lock the lid into place and cook on high pressure for 35 minutes. Manually release the pressure.

5. Meanwhile, in a small bowl, whisk together the ketchup and remaining 1 tablespoon Sriracha to make the glaze.

6. Heat the broiler. Line a small rimmed baking sheet with foil. When the pressure has released, using tongs or mitts, carefully lift the meatloaf pan out of the pressure cooker and transfer to the prepared sheet. Remove the foil from the top of the springform pan. Run a thin offset spatula

or butter knife around the inside edge of the pan, then unmold (or remove meatloaf from the foil). Brush the glaze all over the top and sides of the meatloaf, then broil until the sauce darkens and bubbles, 2 to 4 minutes, watching carefully so the glaze doesn't burn.

7. Mash the potatoes up slightly with a fork if you like, and top with some butter, a drizzle of Sriracha if you like, and some chopped herbs. Serve the potatoes with the meatloaf and more Sriracha on the side.

BEEF + SWEET POTATO GRATIN

ACTIVE TIME: 25 MINUTES
PRESSURE COOK TIME: 35 MINUTES
TOTAL TIME: 55 MINUTES
YIELD: 3 TO 4 SERVINGS

---

1 tablespoon extra-virgin olive oil

1 pound ground beef (preferably 90% lean)

Kosher salt and freshly ground black pepper

1 small onion, halved and thinly sliced

1 green bell pepper, diced

½ cup chopped tomatoes

2 garlic cloves, finely chopped

1 tablespoon chopped fresh sage

2 teaspoons Worcestershire sauce

Butter, for greasing the pan

¾ pound sweet potatoes, peeled and thinly sliced (about 1 large)

1 cup shredded Gruyère or cheddar cheese (4 ounces)

In this supremely comforting dish, a layer of ground beef flavored with onions, peppers, and tomatoes is topped with thinly sliced sweet potatoes and Gruyère cheese before being pressure-cooked until melting soft. Then the dish is sprinkled with more Gruyère and run under the broiler, so the cheese can form a browned and melted cap. Serve it on a cold wintry evening with a crisp green salad—it will warm you through and through.

---

1. Using the sauté function (on high, if possible), heat the oil in the pressure cooker pot. Stir in the meat, ½ teaspoon salt, and ¼ teaspoon pepper and cook, breaking the meat up with a spoon, until no longer pink. Press the meat into an even layer in the pot and let it cook undisturbed until well browned, 7 to 10 minutes, then transfer with a slotted spoon to a plate. Leave the fat in the pot.

2. Stir in the onion, bell pepper, tomatoes, and ¼ teaspoon salt and cook, stirring often, until starting to brown, about 5 minutes. Stir in the garlic and sage and cook for 1 minute. Stir the beef and any juices back into the pot, along with the Worcestershire, and let cook for another 30 seconds. Turn off the sauté function (if the mixture starts to burn, remove the pot from the pressure cooker using oven mitts).

3. Butter a porcelain or ceramic (not glass) 7-inch 1½-quart soufflé dish. Spoon the meat mixture into the dish and press the meat down in an even layer.

4. Place one layer of sweet potato slices over the meat, with the slices overlapping each other (use about one-third of the potatoes). Season lightly with salt and pepper. Sprinkle ⅓ cup of the cheese evenly over the potatoes. Repeat with another one-third of the potatoes and ⅓ cup cheese. Make a third layer of sweet potatoes and reserve the final ⅓ cup cheese to sprinkle on at the end. Press the potatoes down; they'll barely fit into the dish at this point, but will sink as the gratin cooks.

5. Cover the dish with foil. Pour 1½ cups water into the pressure cooker pot (no need to clean it). If your steamer rack has handles, place the soufflé dish on the rack and lower everything into the pressure cooker pot. If your rack does not have handles, first place the rack in the pot, then lower in the soufflé dish using a homemade sling (see page 17).

6. Lock the lid into place and cook on high pressure for 35 minutes. Manually release the pressure.

7. Heat the broiler. Sprinkle the reserved ⅓ cup cheese over the potatoes and broil until golden, 1½ to 3 minutes. Let cool for 5 minutes, then serve, spooning some of the liquid from the bottom of the soufflé dish on top of the potatoes.

GINGERY PORK MEATBALLS WITH SWISS CHARD

ACTIVE TIME: 15 MINUTES
PRESSURE COOK TIME: 5 MINUTES
TOTAL TIME: 50 MINUTES
YIELD: 2 TO 4 SERVINGS

---

2 tablespoons toasted sesame oil

2 shallots or 1 small red onion, diced

3 ounces shiitake mushroom caps, finely chopped (about 1 cup)

1 serrano or jalapeño chile, seeded (if desired) and diced

1 tablespoon finely grated fresh ginger

3 garlic cloves, finely grated or minced

Finely grated zest of 1 lime

2 teaspoons soy sauce

1½ teaspoons Asian fish sauce

Kosher salt

1 pound ground pork or turkey

⅓ cup panko bread crumbs

1 large egg

1 bunch Swiss chard, any tough ribs and stems removed

Cooked white rice, for serving (optional)

Sriracha, for serving (optional)

Lime wedges, for serving

These sesame-flavored meatballs are like the filling of your favorite pork dumplings. But instead of dumpling wrappers, I've layered them in Swiss chard leaves, which turn silky under pressure and add something green and fresh to the meal. If you aren't a Sriracha fan, these are also nice dunked in a little soy sauce flavored with grated ginger and a dash of rice vinegar. You just need something sharp and tangy as a dipping sauce to offset the richness of the meat.

---

1. Using the sauté function, heat the sesame oil in the pressure cooker pot. Stir in the shallots, mushrooms, and chile and cook, stirring frequently, until soft, 3 to 4 minutes. Stir in the ginger and garlic and cook until fragrant, another 1 minute. Scrape into a large bowl and stir in the lime zest, soy sauce, fish sauce, and ½ teaspoon salt.

2. Add the pork, panko, and egg to the mushroom mixture and use your hands to mix until just combined. Try not to overwork the mixture or the meatballs may turn out tough and dense. Roll into 1½-inch balls.

3. Pour 1 cup water into the pressure cooker pot (no need to rinse it out first). Place a steamer basket at the bottom of the pot.

4. Pat the chard leaves dry. Place one or two large chard leaves on the bottom of the steamer basket. Arrange a layer of meatballs on top, spacing them 1 inch apart. Place another layer of leaves on top of the meatballs (so that the meatballs are not visible), then layer more meatballs on top. Continue until you've used up all the meatballs and chard leaves, ending with chard. You should have 3 to 4 layers of meatballs. Season the top layer of chard lightly with salt.

5. Lock the lid into place and cook on high pressure for 5 minutes. Let the pressure release naturally for 10 minutes, then manually release the remaining pressure.

6. Serve the meatballs and chard with rice, if desired. Accompany with Sriracha (if using) and lime wedges.

RED WINE BOLOGNESE

ACTIVE TIME: 25 MINUTES
PRESSURE COOK TIME: 20 MINUTES
TOTAL TIME: 55 MINUTES
YIELD: 4 SERVINGS

---

2 tablespoons unsalted butter

1½ tablespoons extra-virgin olive oil, plus more for drizzling

¾ cup diced onion

1 large celery stalk, finely diced

1 large carrot, finely diced

Kosher salt

1 pound ground beef

¼ teaspoon freshly ground black pepper, plus more if needed

½ cup whole milk

½ cup red wine

1 cup canned diced tomatoes with liquid

12 ounces pasta, cooked according to the package directions, for serving

Freshly grated Parmesan cheese, for serving

COOK IT SLOW

After step 2, slow cook on high for 2 to 3 hours or low for 4 to 6 hours. Proceed with step 4 to thicken the sauce.

This meaty sauce has all the complex flavors of a long-simmered Bolognese, without taking hours to make. I like to serve it over short tubular or twisty pasta rigatoni, penne, or fusilli—so the bits of meat and vegetables can nestle in the crevices. For an untraditional yet wonderfully briny variation, stir in ½ cup sliced green or black olives before you reduce the sauce.

---

1. Using the sauté function, melt the butter and oil in the pressure cooker pot. Stir in the onion, celery, carrot, and a pinch of salt. Cook, stirring occasionally, until the onions are translucent, about 5 minutes.

2. Stir in the beef, 1 teaspoon salt, and the pepper, using a spoon to break up the meat. Press the meat into the bottom of the pot, turn the sauté function to high, if possible, and cook without stirring until there are golden spots on the bottom, 5 to 10 minutes. Stir in the milk, red wine, and tomatoes.

3. Lock the lid into place and cook on high pressure for 20 minutes. Let the pressure release naturally for 5 minutes, then manually release the remaining pressure.

4. Using the sauté function, bring the sauce to a simmer and let it reduce, stirring occasionally, until thickened to taste, 8 to 12 minutes. Taste and add more salt and pepper if needed.

5. Toss with the cooked pasta and serve with a shower of Parmesan cheese and a drizzle of good olive oil.

LAMB + BULGUR
STUFFED PEPPERS WITH YOGURT SAUCE

ACTIVE TIME: 20 MINUTES
PRESSURE COOK TIME: 9 MINUTES
TOTAL TIME: 40 MINUTES
YIELD: 4 SERVINGS

FOR THE PEPPERS

½ cup bulgur

4 red, yellow, or orange bell peppers, or a combination

2 scallions (white and green parts), thinly sliced

2 garlic cloves, finely grated or minced

1 large egg

2 tablespoons chopped fresh dill or parsley

1¼ teaspoons kosher salt

½ teaspoon freshly ground black pepper

¾ teaspoon ground cumin

¼ teaspoon ground allspice

⅛ teaspoon ground cinnamon

Pinch of cayenne pepper (optional)

½ pound ground lamb or lean ground beef

¼ cup crumbled feta cheese

In this Middle Eastern take on stuffed peppers, the filling of ground lamb and tender bulgur is seasoned with feta, dill, and cumin, making it especially savory. If you're not a lamb fan, you can substitute ground turkey or lean ground beef (avoid fattier ground beef or the dish could be greasy). Choose squat bell peppers that stand up by themselves for this; they make the most attractive presentation. If you have extra garlic yogurt sauce, keep it in the fridge and use it as a dip for vegetables. I love it with sliced cucumbers and crackers as a midafternoon snack.

---

1. Prepare the peppers: In a medium heatproof bowl, top the bulgur with enough boiling water to cover by 1 inch. Let it sit while you prepare the rest of the ingredients, about 10 minutes.

2. Pour 1 cup water into the pressure cooker pot. Place a steamer rack/trivet in the bottom.

3. Cut the tops off of the peppers and carefully cut out the ribs and seeds with a paring knife (or grapefruit spoon or melon baller) while keeping the bottom of the pepper intact. Reserve the pepper tops.

4. Drain the bulgur in a fine-mesh sieve, pressing out the excess water, and transfer to a large bowl. Mix in the scallions, garlic, egg, dill, salt, pepper, cumin, allspice, cinnamon, and cayenne (if using). Add the lamb and gently mix with the other ingredients, using a light touch here. You don't want to overwork the meat, which can make the stuffing dense. Fold in the feta cheese.

5. Loosely stuff the peppers with the lamb mixture, taking care not to pack it in, then place the pepper tops over the peppers. Place the peppers on top of the rack/trivet, standing upright.

6. Lock the lid into place and cook on high pressure for 9 minutes. Manually release the pressure.

7. Meanwhile, make the sauce: In a small bowl, mix together the yogurt, dill, garlic, salt, and cayenne (if using).

8. Serve the peppers drizzled with the yogurt sauce, sprinkled with more dill and feta, and with the lemon wedges on the side.

FOR THE YOGURT SAUCE

1 cup plain yogurt

1 tablespoon chopped fresh dill

1 garlic clove, finely grated or minced

¼ teaspoon kosher salt, or more to taste

Pinch of cayenne pepper (optional)

FOR SERVING

Chopped fresh dill or parsley

Crumbled feta cheese

Lemon wedges

SHRIMP + GRITS WITH BACON + CHEDDAR

ACTIVE TIME: 30 MINUTES
PRESSURE COOK TIME: 10 MINUTES
TOTAL TIME: 55 MINUTES
YIELD: 4 SERVINGS

1½ pounds peeled and deveined large shrimp

1½ tablespoons Old Bay seasoning

2 slices smoked bacon, diced

1 small onion, diced

1 small red bell pepper, diced

1 jalapeño chile, seeded (if desired) and diced

2 garlic cloves, thinly sliced

1 14.5-ounce can diced tomatoes

¾ teaspoon kosher salt, plus more if needed

½ cup old-fashioned or stone-ground grits

1 cup whole milk

¾ cup shredded cheddar cheese (3 ounces)

2 tablespoons unsalted butter

½ tablespoon fresh lemon juice

Sliced scallions, for serving

Hot sauce and/or lemon wedges, for serving

This is slightly more involved than other shrimp and grits recipes out there, but the results are worth it. By keeping the grits and shrimp separate until the last minute, you get a wonderful contrast of flavors—a mound of mild, creamy, cheesy grits and a topping of tomatoey, oniony shrimp. The hot sauce for serving is important here—not only does it add heat, it also gives an acidic jolt that really enlivens the sweet shrimp and buttery grits. But a squeeze of lemon works, too, if you like things on the milder side.

---

1. In a large bowl, combine the shrimp and Old Bay seasoning. Cover and let marinate at room temperature while you prepare the remaining ingredients.

2. Using the sauté function, scatter the bacon into the pressure cooker pot and cook, stirring frequently, until browned and the fat has rendered, 10 to 12 minutes. Leaving the fat in the pan, transfer the bacon with a slotted spoon to a plate lined with paper towels.

3. Stir the onion, bell pepper, jalapeño, and garlic into the pot. Cook until softened and translucent, about 5 minutes.

4. Stir in the tomatoes and ½ teaspoon of the salt, scraping up any browned bits on the bottom, and turn off the sauté function.

5. In a medium metal (not glass) bowl that fits in the pressure cooker, stir together the grits, milk, 1 cup water, and remaining ¼ teaspoon salt. If your steamer rack has handles, place the bowl on the rack and lower everything into the pressure cooker pot, setting it over the tomato mixture. If your rack does not have handles, first place the rack in the pot, then lower in the bowl using a homemade sling (see page 17).

6. Lock the lid into place and cook on high pressure for 10 minutes. Let the pressure release naturally.

7. Carefully remove the bowl from the pressure cooker, using the sling or oven mitts. Stir the cheddar and butter into the grits, adding more milk or water to reach your desired consistency. Taste and add more salt if needed.

8. Using the sauté function, stir the marinated shrimp and lemon juice into the tomato mixture in the pressure cooker pot and cook, stirring frequently, until the shrimp are cooked through, 3 to 5 minutes.

9. To serve, spoon the grits onto serving bowls and top with the shrimp and tomato mixture, reserved bacon, scallions, and hot sauce and/or lemon wedges on the side.

SALMON WITH LEMON-CAPER BUTTER

ACTIVE TIME: 5 MINUTES
PRESSURE COOK TIME: 1 MINUTE
TOTAL TIME: 20 MINUTES
YIELD: 4 SERVINGS

---

4 tablespoons (½ stick) unsalted butter, at room temperature

2 tablespoons drained capers, chopped

1 fat garlic clove, finely grated or minced

1 tablespoon finely grated lemon zest (cut the bald lemon into wedges for serving)

¼ teaspoon kosher salt

¼ teaspoon freshly ground black pepper

4 6-ounce skin-on salmon fillets, patted dry

¼ cup dry white wine

Chopped parsley, for serving

If you love salmon and salty, briny capers, meet your new weeknight go-to meal. The lemon-caper butter adds brightness and tang to the wonderfully oily fish, and it all comes together in just 20 minutes. Note that if you use thick, center-cut salmon fillets, they will be slightly dark pink and rare in the center; thinner fillets will cook all the way through. So choose the thickness of your fillets based on your preference for doneness.

---

1. In a small bowl, mash together 3 tablespoons of the butter, the capers, garlic, lemon zest, salt, and pepper. Rub half of the mixture all over the flesh of the salmon (not the skin).

2. Using the sauté function, melt the remaining 1 tablespoon butter in the pressure cooker pot. Place the salmon skin-side down in the pot, then pour in the wine.

3. Lock the lid into place and cook on low pressure for 1 minute. Manually release the pressure.

4. Transfer the salmon to serving plates (if it sticks, use a thin metal spatula to pry it out of the pan). Dollop the salmon with the remaining lemon-caper butter and top with parsley. Serve with the lemon wedges.

COZY COOKING

FOR THE WEEKENDS

FRENCH BEEF DAUBE
WITH OLIVES

ACTIVE TIME: 50 MINUTES
PRESSURE COOK TIME: 20 MINUTES
TOTAL TIME: 1 HOUR 30 MINUTES
YIELD: 8 SERVINGS

---

1 long strip of orange zest, about ½ inch wide (use a vegetable peeler)

3 bay leaves

4 sprigs fresh parsley

6 sprigs fresh thyme

3-inch cinnamon stick

5 ounces sliced bacon, thinly sliced crosswise into batons

3 pounds boneless short ribs or beef stew meat, cut into 1½-inch chunks

1 tablespoon plus 1 teaspoon kosher salt

1 teaspoon freshly ground black pepper

2 onions, thickly sliced

1 fennel bulb, trimmed and sliced (chop the fronds and reserve)

6 garlic cloves, chopped

1 14.5-ounce can diced tomatoes

1½ cups red wine

3 large carrots, halved lengthwise and cut into ½-inch-thick half-moons

4 whole cloves

1 cup black olives, coarsely chopped

½ cup fresh parsley, chopped

Lemon wedges, for serving

Most of the time spent making this elegant, rich stew is in the sautéing and browning stages. Once you add the meat, it will cook until spoonably tender in only 20 minutes. But that sautéing and browning is what yields all the flavor, each step building upon the last to give a heady, winey sauce that you'll want to mop up with a crusty piece of bread or mound of mashed potatoes. Boneless beef short ribs will give you the most flavorful and tender result, but cubed brisket or beef stew meat will also work.

---

1. Tie together the orange zest, bay leaves, parsley sprigs, thyme sprigs, and cinnamon stick with kitchen twine to make a bouquet garni. This will make everything easy to remove after cooking. (If you don't have any kitchen twine, you can just throw everything into the pot, but you'll have to fish it all out or warn your guests before serving.)

2. Using the sauté function, cook the bacon, stirring occasionally, until the fat has rendered and the bacon is crispy, about 10 minutes. Leaving the fat in the pan, transfer the bacon with a slotted spoon to a plate lined with paper towels.

3. Season the beef with 1 tablespoon of the salt and the pepper. Working in batches, arrange the beef in a single layer in the pot and cook until well browned on all sides, 5 to 10 minutes per batch. Transfer the browned beef to a plate as the rest of it cooks.

4. Stir the onions, fennel, garlic, and remaining 1 teaspoon salt into the pot. Cook until soft and most of the liquid has cooked off, 10 to 12 minutes. Stir in the tomatoes and wine, scraping the browned bits from the pot, bring to a simmer, and cook until the liquid has reduced by half, about 15 minutes.

5. Stir in the carrots, cloves, browned beef and any juices, half the bacon, and the bouquet garni.

6. Lock the lid into place and cook on high pressure for 20 minutes. Let the pressure release naturally.

7. Stir in the olives, chopped parsley, and the fennel fronds and serve garnished with the remaining bacon and with lemon wedges for squeezing.

COOK IT SLOW

After step 5, slow cook on high for 7 to 9 hours or low for 10 to 12 hours. If the sauce seems too thin, remove the lid and use the sauté function on high to cook uncovered until thickened to taste.

CHIPOTLE PORK TACOS

ACTIVE TIME: 30 MINUTES
PRESSURE COOK TIME: 45 MINUTES
TOTAL TIME: 1 HOUR 45 MINUTES
YIELD: 8 TO 10 SERVINGS

FOR THE PORK

3 pounds boneless pork shoulder, cut into 4 pieces

2 teaspoons kosher salt, plus more if needed

4 garlic cloves, peeled

1 jalapeño chile, stemmed, halved, and seeded if desired

½ cup fresh orange juice

2 tablespoons apple cider vinegar

2 tablespoons chopped chipotle chile in adobo sauce

1 teaspoon ancho chile powder

1 teaspoon dried oregano, preferably Mexican oregano

1 teaspoon ground cumin

½ teaspoon ground coriander

½ teaspoon freshly ground black pepper

3 tablespoons lard or safflower or other neutral oil

COOK IT SLOW

After step 4, slow cook on high for 7 to 9 hours or low for 10 to 12 hours. If the sauce seems too thin, remove the lid and cook uncovered on high until thickened to taste.

In this succulent pork dish, boneless pork shoulder is pressure-cooked in spicy red chile sauce with orange juice, oregano, and cumin until thoroughly fork tender. Then, right before serving, it's fried until crisp and golden in a skillet on the stove. This last step makes it ideal for cooking ahead and then browning in the pan just before serving. Note that this recipe feeds 8 to 10 people, but if you're not having a party, you can keep it in your fridge for up to a week and reheat it as needed. It's a convenient and extremely tasty meal.

1. Prepare the pork: Season the pork shoulder all over with 1½ teaspoons of the salt and set aside at room temperature for 30 minutes.

2. Meanwhile, using the sauté function (on high, if possible), toast the garlic and jalapeño in the pressure cooker pot (dry, without any oil) until dark brown in spots, turning occasionally, 10 to 12 minutes.

3. Transfer the browned jalapeño and garlic to a blender and add the orange juice, cider vinegar, chipotle chile, ancho powder, oregano, cumin, coriander, black pepper, and the remaining ½ teaspoon salt. Puree until smooth, about 1 minute.

4. Add the pork to the pot (the pot might still be hot, and that's okay). Pour the chile sauce mixture over the pork and toss well to coat the meat all over.

5. Lock the lid into place and cook on high pressure for 45 minutes. Let the pressure release naturally.

6. Use tongs to transfer the meat to a cutting board or metal bowl. Skim the fat off the top of the sauce in the pot. Using the sauté function (on high, if possible), simmer the sauce until it reduces and thickens slightly (it won't be thick, just thicker), 12 to 15 minutes. Taste and add more salt if needed.

7. When the meat is cool enough to handle, shred it into chunks using two forks or your hands, adding any juices back into the pot with the sauce.

8. Just before serving, in a very large skillet, heat the lard or oil over high heat. Add the pork and fry the meat until it is browned at the edges, 5 to 10 minutes. (You may have to do this in batches if the meat doesn't fit in one layer in your pan). Pour ¼ cup of the reduced sauce from the pot into the skillet with the pork and let it sizzle until it evaporates and coats the meat. This is important: The sauce is what makes the dish. Taste and add more sauce if needed.

9. Serve the pork on a platter topped with onion, cilantro, and jalapeño, with more warm sauce on the side. Let your guests build their own tacos, using warm tortillas, avocado and a squeeze of lime, adding more sauce to taste and Cotija cheese, if desired.

FOR SERVING

Thinly sliced white onion

Cilantro leaves

Thinly sliced jalapeño chiles

Tortillas, warmed

Sliced avocado

Lime wedges

Cotija or feta cheese, crumbled (optional)

RED WINE BRISKET WITH PRUNES

ACTIVE TIME: 40 MINUTES
PRESSURE COOK TIME: 60 MINUTES
TOTAL TIME: 2 HOURS 10 MINUTES, PLUS AT LEAST 2 HOURS MARINATING
YIELD: 8 SERVINGS

---

2 garlic cloves, finely grated or minced

2½ teaspoons kosher salt

¾ teaspoon pimentón (smoked hot paprika)

½ teaspoon freshly ground black pepper

¼ teaspoon ground allspice

3 to 3½ pounds beef brisket, cut into 3 or 4 pieces

4 large sprigs fresh thyme

1 to 3 tablespoons olive oil, as needed

1 large white or Spanish onion, diced

1 teaspoon tomato paste

1 cup red wine

3 carrots, cut into 1-inch lengths

¼ cup chopped prunes

1 bay leaf

1 cinnamon stick

One of the more involved dishes in this book, this succulent, tender brisket with its robust and aromatic sauce is well worth the time it takes to prepare. The prunes completely break down under pressure, giving the sauce body and sweetness, while the smoked paprika, cinnamon, and bay leaf make it fragrant and complex. Note that most briskets for sale are very lean (called "first cut"). If you can find "second cut" or "deckle" brisket, it will be fattier and, therefore, richer and more tender. It will also add a lot in terms of beefy flavor. Just be sure to skim the rendered fat extra carefully in step 5 so the sauce isn't greasy. Serve this with buttered noodles if you want to go the full-on comfort food route, or with polenta or roasted potatoes for something a little more sophisticated.

---

1. In a large bowl, combine the garlic, salt, pimentón, black pepper, and allspice. Add the beef to the bowl and rub the garlic mixture all over the meat, then top with the sprigs of thyme. Cover and let rest in the refrigerator for at least 2 hours, or up to 24 hours.

2. Using the sauté function, heat 1 tablespoon of the oil in the pressure cooker pot. Pull the thyme sprigs off the beef and reserve. Working in batches, add the beef to the pot and sear until browned all over, about 2 minutes per side, taking care to brown all sides of the meat, and adding more oil as needed. Transfer the beef to a plate as it's done browning.

3. If the pot looks dry, add a bit more oil. Add the onion and sauté, scraping up the browned bits at the bottom of the pot, until the onions are golden at the edges, about 5 minutes.

4. Add the tomato paste and sauté until it darkens, 1 to 2 minutes. Return the beef to the pot and add the wine, carrots, prunes, bay leaf, cinnamon stick, and reserved thyme sprigs.

5. Lock the lid into place and cook on high pressure for 60 minutes. Let the pressure release naturally for 20 minutes, then manually release the remaining pressure.

6. Transfer the beef to a plate or a carving board, preferably with a juice groove to catch the liquid, and tent with foil to keep warm. Using the sauté function, simmer the remaining sauce in the pressure cooker until it thickens to taste, about 20 minutes. Use a fat-separator to skim the fat, or let the sauce settle and spoon the fat off the top. Remove the bay leaf, cinnamon stick, and thyme sprigs. Add any juices from the cutting board to the sauce.

7. Slice the beef and serve with the sauce alongside.

COOK IT SLOW

Cut the meat into 6 to 8 pieces, marinate and brown as directed in steps 1 and 2, and place the browned meat in the pot. Cover the meat with the onion-carrot mixture from steps 3 and 4. Cook on high for 6 to 8 hours or low for 9 to 11 hours. Proceed with steps 6 and 7.

GINGER SESAME GLAZED SPARE RIBS

ACTIVE TIME: 25 MINUTES
PRESSURE COOK TIME: 34 MINUTES
TOTAL TIME: 1 HOUR 10 MINUTES
YIELD: 4 SERVINGS

---

5 large garlic cloves

2 tablespoons chopped candied ginger

1 tablespoon grated fresh ginger

2 tablespoons light brown sugar

2 tablespoons toasted sesame oil

1 tablespoon sake, white wine, or dry vermouth

2 tablespoons white sesame seeds, plus more for garnish

2 teaspoons gochugaru (Korean chile flakes) or crushed red pepper flakes

1½ teaspoons freshly ground black pepper

½ cup soy sauce

5 pounds pork spare ribs, racks cut into 2 or 3 pieces

Lime wedges, for serving

COOK IT SLOW

Cook the ribs, covered in their sauce, on high for 4 to 5 hours or low for 7 to 8 hours. Proceed with steps 4 through 6 to broil the ribs.

Pork ribs are ideal fodder for the electric pressure cooker. The tough, fibrous flesh will practically melt off the bone in just about 30 minutes, and the pressure helps infuse the meat with the flavor of the sauce. Here, the combination of candied and (plenty of) grated fresh ginger give these sesame spare ribs both sweetness and verve, while Korean chile flakes add a pungent bite. (If you can't find gochugaru, crushed red pepper flakes work well, too.)

If you want to make these in advance, cook the ribs and reduce the sauce up to 3 days ahead, but don't broil them in step 5 until just before serving. The broiler will glaze and reheat at the same time.

---

1. In a mini food processor or blender, puree the garlic, candied ginger, fresh ginger, brown sugar, sesame oil, sake, sesame seeds, gochugaru, and black pepper. Scrape the mixture into a large bowl and whisk in the soy sauce.

2. Toss the ribs with the sauce, then transfer the ribs to the pressure cooker pot, arranging them standing up along the wall of the pot with the meat facing the wall. Continue with the remaining ribs, placing them in concentric circles. Pour any remaining sauce over the ribs.

3. Lock the lid into place and cook on high pressure for 34 minutes. Let the pressure release naturally.

4. Line a rimmed baking sheet with aluminum foil. Arrange the ribs, meat-side down, on the sheet. Using the sauté function, reduce the sauce in the pressure cooker to a thick glaze, 8 to 15 minutes.

5. Meanwhile, heat the broiler.

6. Brush the thickened glaze on the ribs and broil the ribs until they are charred in spots, 2 to 3 minutes. Carefully flip the ribs and brush again with the glaze, then broil until evenly charred, 2 to 4 minutes more. Brush with more glaze and sprinkle with sesame seeds. Serve hot with lime wedges on the side.

SPICY CURRIED LAMB WITH YOGURT

ACTIVE TIME: 25 MINUTES
PRESSURE COOK TIME: 28 MINUTES
TOTAL TIME: 1 HOUR 30 MINUTES
YIELD: 4 TO 6 SERVINGS

---

3 pounds boneless lamb stew meat, cut into 1½-inch chunks

3 teaspoons kosher salt, or more if needed

1½ teaspoons ground garam masala

3 tablespoons neutral oil, such as grapeseed or sunflower

2 small red onions, finely diced

4 garlic cloves, finely grated or minced

1½ teaspoons grated fresh ginger

1¼ teaspoons sweet paprika

1 teaspoon ground coriander

½ teaspoon cayenne pepper

¼ teaspoon ground turmeric

½ cup plain whole-milk Greek yogurt, plus more for serving (optional)

2 medium white or gold potatoes, peeled and cut into 2-inch chunks

¾ pound green beans, trimmed and cut into 1-inch pieces

Cooked rice or naan, for serving

Chopped cilantro, for serving

This homey lamb curry has a creamy sauce thanks both to whole-milk yogurt and to the potatoes that break down as they cook, adding their starch to the mix. The green beans aren't strictly necessary, but they do add a bit of color and texture to an otherwise very soft, very brown dish. You can use any boneless lamb here, which is usually cut from the shoulder or leg. I've used meat labeled for kebabs as successfully as lamb stew meat, so buy whatever is available.

---

1. Season the lamb with 2 teaspoons of the salt and ½ teaspoon of the garam masala and let it sit for 30 minutes.

2. Using the sauté function, heat the oil in the pressure cooker pot. Stir in the onions and remaining 1 teaspoon salt and cook, stirring very frequently, until browned, 12 to 15 minutes. Stir in the garlic, ginger, paprika, coriander, cayenne, turmeric, and remaining 1 teaspoon garam masala and cook for 1 minute.

3. Turn off the sauté function. Stir in the yogurt, 1 heaping spoonful at a time, mixing well with each addition to discourage curdling. Stir in the lamb and potatoes.

4. Lock the lid into place and cook on high pressure for 28 minutes. Manually release the pressure.

5. Uncover, turn on the sauté function, and bring to a simmer. Stir in the green beans and simmer until just tender, 3 to 5 minutes. Taste and add more salt if needed. Serve with rice or naan, and topped with cilantro and yogurt, if you like.

COOK IT SLOW

After step 3, cook on high for 5 to 7 hours or low for 8 to 10 hours. Add the green beans during the last 15 minutes of cooking.

COOK IT SLOW

After step 2, slow cook on high for 4 to 5 hours or low for 7 to 8 hours. In the last 20 minutes of cooking, add the sausage and cook uncovered. The beans and liquid should thicken in this time.

CAJUN RED BEANS WITH ANDOUILLE SAUSAGE

ACTIVE TIME: 25 MINUTES
PRESSURE COOK TIME: 15 MINUTES
TOTAL TIME: 1 HOUR 15 MINUTES, PLUS 6 HOURS SOAKING
YIELD: 6 TO 8 SERVINGS

---

2 tablespoons extra-virgin olive oil

1 pound andouille sausage, sliced

1 large onion, diced

1 green bell pepper, diced

1 red bell pepper, diced

2 celery stalks, diced (leaves reserved for garnish)

5 fat garlic cloves, sliced, plus 1 clove finely grated or minced

2¼ teaspoons kosher salt, plus more if needed

1½ teaspoons chopped fresh sage

½ teaspoon freshly ground black pepper

¼ teaspoon cayenne pepper

3 bay leaves

4 sprigs fresh thyme

1 pound dried kidney beans, soaked in water for at least 6 hours or overnight and drained

Fresh lemon juice

Cooked white rice, for serving

Thinly sliced scallions, for serving

Hot sauce, for serving

This classic Cajun dish cooks up perfectly spicy and meaty in your electric pressure cooker. Serve it over rice doused with hot sauce for a fiery, hearty meal. If you can't find andouille sausage, substitute your favorite full-flavored sausage—even Italian links are fine to use. As long as it has a kick, it will work here. Note that you need to soak the beans for at least 6 hours or overnight before making this dish, so plan ahead.

---

1. Using the sauté function, heat the oil in the pressure cooker pot. Stir in the sausage and cook until well browned, 5 to 7 minutes. Use a slotted spoon to transfer the sausage to a plate.

2. Stir in the onion, bell peppers, celery, sliced garlic, 1 teaspoon of the salt, the sage, black pepper, and cayenne. Cook until the vegetables are soft and just starting to brown, about 7 minutes. Stir in the bay leaves, thyme, beans, 3½ cups water, and remaining 1¼ teaspoons salt.

3. Lock the lid into place and cook on high pressure for 15 minutes. Let the pressure release naturally.

4. Remove the thyme sprigs and bay leaves. Use a slotted spoon to remove two-thirds of the beans, and set them aside. With an immersion or regular blender, puree the remaining beans in the pot to thicken the mixture.

5. Turn on the sauté function. Stir in the sausage and the reserved beans, bring the entire mixture to a simmer, and cook for 3 to 5 minutes, or until the mixture has thickened to your liking.

6. Taste and add more salt if needed and season with lemon juice to taste. Serve the beans and sausage over rice, topped with scallions, chopped celery leaves, and hot sauce.

BO SSAM

ACTIVE TIME: 25 MINUTES
PRESSURE COOK TIME: 90 MINUTES
TOTAL TIME: 2 HOURS 30 MINUTES, PLUS AT LEAST 6 HOURS MARINATING
YIELD: 12 SERVINGS

Chef David Chang's *bo ssam*—Korean marinated and roasted pork shoulder—is one of the great recipes of the last decade. When the whole shoulder, burnished and glazed on the outside, nearly pudding-soft within, emerges from the oven, it's about as big a triumph as a home cook can hope to achieve. Porky, sweet and salty, and very brawny, it sometimes gets served with a zingy ginger scallion sauce that counters the richness of the meat.

Even better, it's easy to make. The only downside is that in addition to the overnight marinating time, the shoulder needs 6 hours in the oven to cook. But with an electric pressure cooker, that time is reduced to 90 minutes, plus 5 or so minutes under the broiler to crisp the skin. The moist environment of the pressure cooker means that the exterior of the meat doesn't get quite as deeply browned as the original recipe, but it's still wonderfully crunchy and deeply flavorful.

Note that the meat can sometimes fall apart after pressure-cooking. I don't mind this—it may look less impressive than a whole shoulder, but you do get more surface area for the sticky, crunchy crust to form during the broil. However, if you want the impressive look of a whole shoulder, you can substitute an 8- to 9-pound bone-in piece for the boneless chunks of meat and pressure-cook it for 110 minutes. Then check the meat; if it's not quite tender, continue cooking for 10 minutes longer. Timing can vary depending upon the shape of the shoulder and the size of the bone.

Because the sodium content of different salt brands varies, make sure to use Diamond Crystal coarse kosher salt here.

FOR THE PORK

½ cup granulated sugar

½ cup plus 1 tablespoon Diamond Crystal coarse kosher salt

7 to 8 pounds boneless pork shoulder, cut into 3 pieces

7 tablespoons dark brown sugar

FOR THE GINGER SCALLION SAUCE

2½ cups finely chopped scallions (about 2 large bunches), white and green parts

½ cup minced fresh ginger

¼ cup neutral oil, such as grapeseed or sunflower

1½ teaspoons soy sauce, or more to taste

1 teaspoon sherry vinegar, or more to taste

½ teaspoon kosher salt, or more to taste

---

1. Prepare the pork: In a baking dish, combine the granulated sugar and ½ cup of the salt. Add the pork and rub all over with the mixture. Marinate in the refrigerator, uncovered, for at least 6 hours or up to overnight.

2. Pour ½ cup water into the pressure cooker pot. Place a steamer rack/trivet in the bottom. Set the pork on the rack.

3. Lock the lid into place and cook on high pressure for 90 minutes. Let the pressure release naturally. Place a wire rack on a rimmed baking sheet and transfer the pork to the rack.

4. While the pork is cooking, make the ginger scallion sauce: In a medium bowl, stir together the scallions, ginger, oil, soy sauce, sherry vinegar, and salt. Taste and adjust seasoning if necessary, adding more salt, vinegar, or soy sauce to taste.

5. Heat the broiler with a rack in the lower third of the oven. In a medium bowl, mix together the remaining 1 tablespoon salt and the dark brown sugar. Rub the mixture all over the pork, then broil until caramelized and crisp, 3 to 5 minutes per side.

6. Remove the pork from the oven and let cool slightly before transferring to a serving platter. Serve with ginger scallion sauce on the side.

BRAISED LAMB SHANKS
WITH HERBS + GARLIC

ACTIVE TIME: 40 MINUTES
PRESSURE COOK TIME: 45 MINUTES
TOTAL TIME: 2 HOURS, PLUS 4 HOURS MARINATING
YIELD: 4 SERVINGS

---

2 teaspoons kosher salt, plus more if needed

1½ teaspoons sweet paprika

1 teaspoon freshly ground black pepper

½ teaspoon ground coriander

¼ teaspoon cayenne pepper

4 lamb shanks (4 to 5 pounds total)

1 tablespoon extra-virgin olive oil, plus more as needed

1 very large sweet or red onion, halved and thinly sliced

1 fennel bulb, trimmed and thinly sliced

6 garlic cloves, coarsely chopped

1 teaspoon tomato paste

½ cup dry white wine

⅓ cup chicken stock or vegetable broth, preferably homemade (page 108), or water

3 sprigs fresh rosemary

1 bunch scallions, finely chopped

1 cup chopped fresh cilantro

1 cup chopped fresh parsley

½ cup chopped fresh mint or dill

Fresh lemon juice

Lemon wedges, for serving

Meaty lamb shanks are perfect for braising in your pressure cooker. The marrow in the bones seasons the sauce, deepening its flavor, while the meat softens into perfect tenderness. Here, the shanks are cooked with plenty of fresh herbs, wine, and garlic, turning brawny and fragrant. I love this over Herbed Baby Potatoes (page 139), but the Turkish Bulgur Pilaf with Pistachios and Currants (page 132) would add a slightly chewy texture and a touch of sweetness to the plate.

---

1. In a large bowl, mix together the salt, paprika, black pepper, coriander, and cayenne. Rub this mixture all over the lamb shanks, then cover the bowl with plastic wrap and let marinate for at least 4 hours or up to 24 hours in the refrigerator.

2. Using the sauté function, heat the oil in the pressure cooker pot. (Or, if the shanks are too long to fit in your pressure cooker, you can use a large skillet over medium heat.) Working in batches, sear the lamb, adding more oil as needed. Take your time with this, making sure to brown the lamb on all sides, 3 to 5 minutes per side. Transfer the lamb to a plate as it finishes browning.

3. Add the onion and fennel to the pot (or pan), adding a little more olive oil if it looks dry. Cook until tender and lightly browned at the edges, about 5 minutes. Add the garlic and tomato paste and cook until the garlic is very fragrant, 1 to 2 minutes longer. Pour in the wine and stock, add the rosemary sprigs, and bring the liquid to a simmer, scraping up the browned bits on the bottom of the pot. Return the seared lamb and any juices to the pot (or, if you used a skillet, transfer its contents, with the lamb, to the pressure cooker pot).

4. In a small bowl, toss together the scallions and chopped herbs. Sprinkle the lamb with half the herb mixture (reserve the remaining herb mixture for later).

5. Lock the lid into place and cook on high pressure for 45 minutes. Let the pressure release naturally for 15 minutes, then manually release the remaining pressure.

6. Transfer the shanks to a serving platter and cover with foil to keep warm. If you like, at this point you could tear the meat off the bones, or serve it bone-in.

7. Using the sauté function (on high, if possible), bring the liquid in the pot to a simmer. Let simmer until thickened slightly, 8 to 15 minutes. Taste and add more salt, if needed, and a big squeeze or two of lemon juice.

8. Pour the sauce over the lamb and garnish with the reserved chopped herbs and lemon wedges for squeezing.

COOK IT SLOW

After step 4, slow cook on high for 7 to 9 hours or low for 10 to 12 hours. Proceed with steps 6 through 8.

SPICY ASIAN CHICKEN WINGS

ACTIVE TIME: 25 MINUTES
PRESSURE COOK TIME: 3 MINUTES
TOTAL TIME: 1 HOUR 15 MINUTES
YIELD: 6 TO 8 SERVINGS

FOR THE MARINATED WINGS

2 tablespoons soy sauce

2 large garlic cloves, finely grated or minced

½-inch piece fresh ginger, finely grated

½ teaspoon kosher salt

½ teaspoon freshly ground black pepper

2½ to 3 pounds chicken wings

FOR THE GLAZE

1 cup mirin

3 tablespoons Sriracha or other hot sauce

Finely grated zest and juice of 2 limes

2 tablespoons soy sauce

1 tablespoon Asian fish sauce

1 teaspoon ground black pepper

FOR FINISHING AND SERVING

Toasted sesame oil, for drizzling

1 teaspoon sesame seeds, for serving

Fresh ground black pepper, for serving

Chopped scallions or cilantro, for serving

This recipe hits all the right notes—spicy from the hot sauce and fresh ginger, salty from the soy sauce, funky from the fish sauce, sweet from the mirin. Make sure to serve the wings as hot as your fingers can bear. As the sauce cools, it can get a little gloppy, and the wings themselves will lose some of their lovely crunch. But when served steaming hot, they are hard to stop eating—and the second one tastes even better than the first.

---

1. Marinate the wings: In a large bowl, mix together the soy sauce, garlic, ginger, salt, and pepper. Add the chicken and toss to coat. Marinate the chicken for 30 minutes at room temperature or overnight in the refrigerator.

2. Make the glaze: Combine the mirin, Sriracha, lime zest and juice, soy sauce, fish sauce, and pepper in the pressure cooker pot. Using the sauté function, simmer the glaze, stirring frequently, until it reduces enough to coat the back of a spoon, about 8 minutes. Transfer about one-third of the glaze to a large bowl. Transfer another one-third to a small bowl. Reserve both bowls of glaze for later. Leave the last one-third of the glaze in the pot.

3. Add the chicken to the pot with the glaze, along with any liquid from the marinade bowl and 2 tablespoons water.

4. Lock the lid into place and cook on high pressure for 3 minutes. Manually release the pressure.

5. Preheat the broiler to high. Line a rimmed baking sheet with aluminum foil.

6. To finish: Using a slotted spoon or tongs, transfer the chicken wings to the glaze in the large bowl and toss well (discard any liquid still in the pressure cooker pot). Arrange the wings in a single layer on the prepared baking sheet. Drizzle the wings with some sesame oil (about a tablespoon or so, but you don't have to measure it). Broil until they are crispy and browned, 2 to 4 minutes.

7. Transfer the wings to a serving platter and drizzle with the glaze from the small bowl. Garnish with the sesame seeds, pepper, and scallions. Serve hot.

CLASSIC BUFFALO WINGS VARIATION

Marinate the wings in ⅓ cup Tabasco or other hot sauce for 15 minutes or overnight in the fridge. Cook the wings with the marinade for 3 minutes on high pressure, then toss the wings in a mixture of 4 tablespoons melted butter and ¼ cup Tabasco until well coated. Spread the chicken out on a baking sheet to broil, being sure to save the leftover butter sauce in the bowl. Broil the wings, then toss again in the butter sauce mixture. Serve with Blue Cheese Dip (below).

BLUE CHEESE DIP

In a small bowl, mix together ½ cup crumbled blue cheese (about 2 ounces), ⅓ cup sour cream, ¼ cup mayonnaise, 2 tablespoons chopped fresh dill or parsley, 2 teaspoons fresh lemon juice, 1 small garlic clove, finely grated or minced, and salt and pepper to taste.

SOUPS
WILL ALWAYS
COMFORT YOU

BONE BROTH
OR STOCK

ACTIVE TIME: 10 MINUTES
PRESSURE COOK TIME: 1 TO 5 HOURS
TOTAL TIME: 1 HOUR TO 5 HOURS
YIELD: 3 QUARTS

---

3 pounds bones, preferably a mix of meaty bones and marrow-filled bones

3 tablespoons apple cider vinegar (for bone broth only)

1½ tablespoons coarse sea salt, or to taste

1 to 2 celery stalks, to taste

1 large carrot

1 large onion, 2 leeks, or a bunch of leek greens

1 whole clove or star anise pod

2 to 6 garlic cloves, to taste

About 6 sprigs fresh thyme or dill

About 6 sprigs fresh parsley

1 bay leaf

1 teaspoon black peppercorns

2 to 4 coins (1-inch-thick) peeled fresh ginger (optional)

If you recognize this recipe from *Dinner in an Instant,* I hope that means that you, like me, have found that it's worth the time and freezer space to have on hand. If you're new to homemade stock and broth, I hope you become a convert, too. It really gives a dish a depth of flavor that isn't quite the same with the store-bought stuff.

The difference between bone broth and regular broth, or stock, comes down to the length of the cooking time and the addition of acid to the cooking liquid. They taste very similar, though the bone broth has a slightly more intense flavor and a thicker, silkier texture than stock. They can be used interchangeably in recipes.

The bigger difference between the two is in the perceived health benefits. Many people consider bone broth to be therapeutic. The longer cooking time of a bone broth allows the collagen and minerals from the bones and connective tissue to dissolve into the liquid. This process is aided by adding a bit of acid to the pot—in this case, apple cider vinegar—which also helps the bones break down (at the end of cooking, the bones should crumble if you press on them). Note that if you are making a regular stock instead of a bone broth you should omit the vinegar.

Bone broths need ample cooking time for all this to occur, at least 24 to 48 hours when simmered conventionally on the stove or in a slow cooker. Regular stocks cook much more quickly; 2 to 4 hours is all you need on the stove.

But whether you are making bone broth or regular stock, the pressure cooker does the job much faster. Regular stocks will be ready in only an hour or two, while bone broths will be ready in an afternoon.

You can use any bones to make bone broth or stock. I usually use a combination of chicken bones left over from roasted birds (I keep them stored in the freezer) and fresh, meaty pork and beef soup bones that I get from the farmers' market (you can also find them in the supermarket or at a butcher shop). But after the holidays one year, I used a goose carcass, and around Thanksgiving, turkey will likely be the bones of choice. Feel free to mix and match all manner of meat and fowl. Or if you want to make a particular kind of stock—say, chicken or beef—use bones only from that animal.

Roasting the bones before adding them to the pot caramelizes them and makes a much richer and better tasting broth. But for a light chicken stock you could skip that step.

---

1. If you want to roast the bones first, preheat the oven to 450°F. Lay the bones out on a rimmed baking sheet and roast until well browned, 25 to 35 minutes.

2. Put the bones (roasted or not) in the pressure cooker pot and add all the remaining ingredients. (Omit vinegar if making regular stock.) Cover with 3 to 3½ quarts water (the water shouldn't come more than two-thirds of the way up the side of the pot).

3. To make bone broth: For poultry bones, cook on high pressure for 3 hours. For beef, pork, or mixed bones, cook on high pressure for 4¼ hours. You'll know when the bone broth has cooked long enough if all the connective tissue, tendons, and cartilage have dissolved and the bones crumble a bit when you poke at them. If this hasn't happened, cook on high pressure for another 30 minutes and check it again.

4. To make regular stock: If using all chicken or poultry bones, cook on high pressure for 60 minutes. If using beef or pork bones (or a combination of poultry and meat), cook on high pressure for 2 hours.

5. Let the pressure release naturally. Strain the liquid, discarding the solids. Use the broth or stock right away, or store it in the refrigerator or freezer. Bone broth and regular stock will keep for 5 days refrigerated or up to 6 months frozen.

COOK IT SLOW

Cook on low for 10 to 12 hours for regular stock, and 24 to 48 hours for bone broth.

TO MAKE VEGETABLE BROTH:

In the pressure cooker, combine 3 sliced onions and/or leeks, 3 sliced carrots, 3 sliced celery stalks with leaves, 2 garlic cloves, 1 halved plum tomato, 1 bay leaf, 1 teaspoon peppercorns, a large pinch of sea salt, 4 parsley sprigs, and a cup or so of mushrooms, if you have them. Add water to cover by 2 inches, lock the lid in place, and cook on high pressure for 20 minutes. Let the pressure release naturally. Strain the liquid, discarding the solids.

NOTE: BAHARAT is a Middle Eastern spice blend. You can buy it at specialty markets or make your own. To make it, combine:

2 tablespoons sweet paprika
1 tablespoon ground coriander
1 tablespoon ground cumin
1 tablespoon ground turmeric
2 teaspoons ground black pepper
1 teaspoon freshly grated nutmeg
1 teaspoon ground cardamom
½ teaspoon ground allspice

MIDDLE EASTERN RED LENTIL, BEAN + BARLEY SOUP

ACTIVE TIME: 20 MINUTES
PRESSURE COOK TIME: 18 MINUTES
TOTAL TIME: 55 MINUTES
YIELD: 6 TO 8 SERVINGS

---

1 bunch cilantro, leaves and stems separated

3 tablespoons extra-virgin olive oil, plus more for drizzling

2 leeks (white and light green parts only), halved lengthwise and thinly sliced into half-moons

1 small fennel bulb, trimmed and diced

3 garlic cloves, finely grated or minced

2 tablespoons baharat spice blend

⅛ teaspoon cayenne pepper, plus more if needed

½ cinnamon stick

2 tablespoons tomato paste

2 quarts vegetable broth or chicken stock, preferably homemade (page 109)

1 pound (1½ cups) dried navy beans

½ cup pearl barley

2½ teaspoons kosher salt, plus more if needed

2 cups peeled and diced butternut squash

¾ cup peeled and diced turnip

½ cup red lentils

Fresh lemon juice

Yogurt, for serving (optional)

There's a lot going on in this aromatic soup, which is seasoned with a Middle Eastern spice blend called *baharat*. You can buy it at spice shops or make your own (see Note, opposite). Once you have it on hand, you'll probably find yourself using it anywhere you want to add a heady and complex mix of spices: on roasted chicken, eggs, other bean dishes, even avocado toast. Or keep it around just to make this soup, which, with its diversely textured combination of grains, beans, lentils, and plenty of sweet vegetables—winter squash, turnips, and fennel—has become an absolute favorite in our house.

---

1. Finely chop the cilantro stems and set the leaves aside.

2. Using the sauté function (on high, if possible), heat the oil in the pressure cooker pot. Stir in the leeks and cook until they start to brown, about 5 minutes. Stir in the chopped cilantro stems, fennel, and garlic and cook for another 2 minutes. Stir in the baharat, cayenne, cinnamon stick, and tomato paste and cook until caramelized, another 2 minutes. Stir in the broth, beans, barley, and salt.

3. Lock the lid into place and cook on high pressure for 15 minutes. Drape a kitchen towel over the vent, then manually release the pressure. (This prevents the brothy steam from splattering everywhere.)

4. Working quickly, so as not to lose too much heat from the pot, stir in the butternut squash, turnip, and lentils. Lock the lid into place and cook on high pressure for 3 minutes. Draping the vent with a towel again, manually release the pressure.

5. Stir in a squeeze of lemon juice, then taste and add more lemon, salt, and cayenne if needed. Ladle the soup into serving bowls and top with yogurt, if you like, cilantro leaves, and a drizzle of oil.

GREEN CHILE CHICKEN SOUP WITH HOMINY

ACTIVE TIME: 15 MINUTES
PRESSURE COOK TIME: 8 MINUTES
TOTAL TIME: 40 MINUTES (OR LONGER IF [illegible] HOMINY, SEE NOTE)
YIELD: 6 TO 8 SERVINGS

1 tablespoon extra virgin olive oil

1 small onion, halved and thinly sliced

2 jalapeño chiles, seeded and thinly sliced

Kosher salt

2 garlic cloves, minced

1 tablespoon tomato paste

1 teaspoon ancho chile powder

½ teaspoon ground cumin

½ teaspoon dried oregano

2 4.5-ounce cans green chiles, drained

2 quarts chicken stock, preferably homemade (page 108)

4 boneless, skinless chicken thighs

3½ cups cooked hominy, homemade (see Note) or 2 14-ounce cans

1 to 2 teaspoons fresh lime juice, to taste

½ cup chopped fresh cilantro leaves and tender stems

Diced avocado, for serving (optional)

Mexican style chicken soup, simmered with cumin, chiles, and tomatoes. [illegible] is robust and hearty and makes for a more satisfying meal than the typical brothier chicken soup. Some versions call for tortillas to be added to the bowl for bulk. This one has hominy, which contributes a subtle corn flavor and distinctly chewy, pillowy texture that I absolutely adore. But if you can't get it, white beans make an earthy, soft substitute.

---

1. Using the sauté function, heat the oil in the pressure cooker pot. Stir in the onion, jalapeños, and a pinch of salt and cook until translucent, about 4 minutes. Stir in the garlic, tomato paste, ancho powder, cumin, and oregano, and cook for another 1 minute.

2. Stir in the canned green chiles, stock, chicken, 1 teaspoon salt, and 1 cup water.

3. Lock the lid into place and cook on high pressure for 8 minutes. Drape a kitchen towel over the vent, then manually release the pressure. (This prevents the brothy steam from splattering everywhere.)

4. Using tongs, transfer the chicken to a plate. Let it cool, then shred the chicken.

5. Meanwhile, stir in the hominy and lime juice. Set to sauté and bring to a simmer.

6. Stir in the shredded chicken and cilantro. Taste and adjust the seasoning if necessary. Serve with avocado, if you like.

NOTE: TO COOK HOMINY, combine 1 pound dried hominy and ½ teaspoon salt with enough water to cover by 1 inch, and soak for at least 4 hours or overnight. Drain the hominy, then add to the pressure cooker pot along with 6 cups water and 1 teaspoon kosher salt. Cook on high pressure for 70 minutes. Let the pressure release naturally.

ITALIAN BUTTERNUT SQUASH + POTATO SOUP

ACTIVE TIME: 20 MINUTES
PRESSURE COOK TIME: 20 MINUTES
TOTAL TIME: 1 HOUR 25 MINUTES
YIELD: 4 TO 6 SERVINGS

Thick, stew-like, and flecked with red pepper flakes and piney bits of rosemary, this squash soup is spicier, chunkier, and more savory than many of its ilk. If you have a special olive oil that you only pull out for drizzling, this is a good place to use it right at the end.

---

1 tablespoon extra-virgin olive oil, plus more for drizzling

2 tablespoons unsalted butter

2 large or 3 small leeks, halved lengthwise and thinly sliced

2 teaspoons kosher salt, plus more if needed

1 butternut squash (2½ to 3 pounds), peeled, seeded, and cut into 1-inch cubes

2 garlic cloves, finely grated or minced

2 teaspoons chopped fresh rosemary

1 teaspoon chopped fresh thyme

¼ teaspoon crushed red pepper flakes, plus more (optional) for serving

1 large potato (about 8 ounces), peeled and diced

1 quart vegetable broth or chicken stock, preferably homemade (see page 109)

Freshly grated Parmesan cheese, for serving

Lemon wedges, for serving

---

1. Using the sauté function, heat the oil and butter in the pressure cooker pot. Stir in the leeks and 1 teaspoon of the salt and cook until the leeks are soft, about 5 minutes. Add the squash, garlic, rosemary, thyme, red pepper flakes, and remaining 1 teaspoon salt. Cook, stirring occasionally, until the squash begins to brown, about 8 minutes.

2. Add the potato and stock, scraping up the browned bits at the bottom of the pot.

3. Lock the lid into place and cook on high pressure for 20 minutes. Let the pressure release naturally.

4. With an immersion or regular blender, just barely puree the soup, leaving it mostly chunky. Taste and add more salt if needed, keeping in mind that it will be served with salty Parmesan cheese. Ladle the soup into bowls, top with the Parmesan, drizzle with oil, and top with more red pepper flakes if you like. Serve with lemon wedges on the side to add brightness right at the last minute.

COOK IT SLOW

After step 2, slow cook on high for 2 to 3 hours or low for 4 to 5 hours. You may not need to puree the soup at all if the squash has broken down considerably.

CLASSIC MATZO BALL SOUP

ACTIVE TIME: 25 MINUTES
PRESSURE COOK TIME: 13 TO 16 MINUTES
TOTAL TIME: 55 MINUTES, PLUS 1 HOUR CHILLING
YIELD: 4 SERVINGS

FOR THE MATZO BALLS

2 large eggs, lightly beaten

2 tablespoons schmaltz or neutral oil, such as grapeseed or sunflower

2 tablespoons chicken stock, preferably homemade (page 108)

½ cup matzo meal

1 tablespoon finely chopped fresh parsley, plus more for serving

1 fat garlic clove, finely grated or minced

½ teaspoon kosher salt

Pinch of cayenne pepper

Pinch of freshly grated nutmeg

FOR THE SOUP

2 tablespoons schmaltz or neutral oil

1 large onion, diced

2 celery stalks, thinly sliced

Kosher salt

2 carrots, thinly sliced

2 quarts chicken stock, preferably homemade (page 108)

When it comes to cooking matzo balls, there are two schools of thought. Some people like to simmer them in their own pot of stock or heavily salted water and then add them to the soup bowls for serving. This gives you the clearest soup, without the starch of the matzo balls clouding the broth. Others go the simpler route, cooking the balls directly in the soup pot. This recipe follows the latter, easier path. The broth does get a bit cloudy, but the flavor is not impacted, and I'll go for ease over looks any day.

If you do, however, want a crystal-clear broth, you can make the soup, remove it from the pressure cooker pot, then cook the matzo balls in plain chicken stock or 2 quarts well-salted water on high pressure for 13 minutes. Use a slotted spoon to remove the matzo balls after cooking, then add them to the soup just before serving.

---

1. Make the matzo balls: In a large bowl, stir together the eggs, schmaltz, chicken stock, matzo meal, parsley, garlic, salt, cayenne, and nutmeg. Refrigerate, uncovered, until very cold, at least 1 hour or up to overnight.

2. Make the soup: Using the sauté function, heat the schmaltz in the pressure cooker pot. Stir in the onion, celery, and a pinch of salt and cook until softened and translucent, about 5 minutes. Stir in the carrots and stock and bring to a simmer. Keep the sauté function on while you form the matzo balls.

3. Wet your hands and form matzo balls the size of golf balls. Slip them directly into the pot as you make them. You should have 11 or 12 balls.

4. Lock the lid into place and cook on high pressure for 13 minutes. Drape a kitchen towel over the vent and manually release the pressure. (This prevents the brothy steam from splattering everywhere.) Check a matzo ball to make sure it's cooked all the way through. If not, lock the lid back into place and cook on high pressure for another 2 to 3 minutes.

5. To serve, ladle 2 or 3 balls into serving bowls, along with the soup. Sprinkle with fresh parsley.

BROCCOLI + CHEDDAR SOUP

ACTIVE TIME: 25 MINUTES
PRESSURE COOK TIME: 5 MINUTES
TOTAL TIME: [illegible] MINUTES
YIELD: 4 SERVINGS

6 tablespoons unsalted butter

1 large onion, diced

3 garlic cloves, finely grated or minced

Kosher salt and freshly ground black pepper

¼ cup all-purpose flour

¼ teaspoon freshly grated nutmeg

⅛ teaspoon cayenne pepper, plus more to taste

2½ cups chicken stock or vegetable broth, preferably homemade (page 108)

2 pounds broccoli, cut into bite-size pieces (about 16 cups)

1 cup whole milk

2 cups shredded extra-sharp cheddar cheese (8 ounces), plus more for serving

---

The broccoli, some pureed into the broth, some left as florets, makes this healthful; the cheese and milk make it luxuriously creamy. It's a soothing, warming meal that comes together quickly and will disappear just as fast. Use an extra-sharp cheddar here for the deepest flavor.

---

1. Using the sauté function, melt 3 tablespoons of the butter in the pressure cooker pot. Stir in the onion, garlic, and a pinch each of salt and pepper. Cook until softened, about 5 minutes. Scoop out the onion mixture with a slotted spoon and transfer to a bowl. Set aside.

2. Melt the remaining 3 tablespoons butter in the pot, then whisk in the flour, nutmeg, and cayenne and cook, stirring constantly, until lightly browned, 1 to 2 minutes. Whisk in the stock, stirring constantly, until smooth and free of lumps. Then stir in 1 teaspoon salt, the cooked onion mixture, and the broccoli.

3. Lock the lid into place and cook on high pressure for 5 minutes. Drape a kitchen towel over the vent, then manually release the pressure. (This prevents the brothy steam from splattering everywhere.)

4. Use a slotted spoon to scoop out 1 cup of the broccoli florets (leave the stem pieces in the pot) and set aside. Stir the milk and 2 cups Cheddar cheese into the pot. With an immersion blender, puree the soup to the desired consistency (or transfer to a regular blender).

5. Stir in the reserved broccoli florets. Taste and season with more salt or pepper if needed. Serve topped with more cheddar.

SWEET POTATO MISO SOUP WITH TOFU + SPINACH

ACTIVE TIME: 15 MINUTES
PRESSURE COOK TIME: 2 MINUTES
TOTAL TIME: 30 MINUTES
YIELD: 4 TO 6 SERVINGS

---

1 tablespoon toasted sesame oil, plus more for drizzling

4 scallions, sliced, white and green parts kept separate

3½ ounces (about 3 cups) shiitake mushrooms, stems discarded and caps thinly sliced

1-inch piece fresh ginger, peeled

Kosher salt

1 quart chicken stock or vegetable broth, preferably homemade (page 108)

1 large sweet potato, peeled and cut into ¾-inch chunks

2 cups baby spinach, torn

1 4 x 5-inch piece kombu

¼ cup white or yellow miso, plus more if needed

7 ounces firm tofu (about ½ block), cut into chunks

This colorful, healthful soup combines cubes of springy tofu and velvety sweet potato with shiitake mushrooms and plenty of spinach. It's flavorful and light, yet still extremely satisfying. Kombu, a type of dried Japanese seaweed available at gourmet markets and specialty shops, adds an umami depth of flavor here. But if you can't find it, leave it out, though you'll probably have to add a bit more miso and salt to make up for the lack.

---

1. Using the sauté function (on low, if possible), heat the oil in the pressure cooker pot. Stir in the scallion whites, most of the greens (reserve a couple tablespoons for garnish), the mushrooms, ginger, and a pinch of salt. Cook until the vegetables are softened but not browning, 2 to 4 minutes.

2. Add the stock, 2 cups water, the sweet potato, spinach, and ½ teaspoon salt. Place the kombu on top of everything.

3. Lock the lid into place and cook on high pressure for 2 minutes. Drape a kitchen towel over the vent, then manually release the pressure. (This prevents the brothy steam from splattering everywhere.)

4. Remove the kombu and either discard or chop into pieces and set aside. Ladle about ½ cup soup into a medium bowl and whisk in the miso. Stir the miso mixture back into the pot. Add the tofu and reserved chopped kombu, if using, and taste, stirring in more miso and salt if needed. To serve, ladle into bowls and top with the reserved scallion greens and a drizzle of sesame oil.

SWEET POTATO MISO SOUP
WITH TOFU + SPINACH

LEBANESE CHICKEN SOUP

ACTIVE TIME: 25 MINUTES
PRESSURE COOK TIME: 8 MINUTES
TOTAL TIME: 1 HOUR 10 MINUTES
YIELD: 6 TO 8 SERVINGS

---

4 tablespoons (½ stick) unsalted butter

1 Vidalia or other sweet onion, diced

1 shallot, diced

1 cup vermicelli or angel hair noodles (break them up with your hands so they fit into a measuring cup)

1 cinnamon stick

2 teaspoons kosher salt, plus more if needed

1 teaspoon freshly ground black pepper

1 teaspoon ground allspice

½ teaspoon ground cardamom

½ teaspoon ground cumin

⅛ teaspoon freshly grated nutmeg

4 sprigs fresh parsley

2 large sprigs fresh rosemary

4 sprigs fresh thyme

3 carrots, diced

4 boneless, skinless chicken thighs

1 quart chicken stock, preferably homemade (page 108)

¾ cup long-grain white rice

1 cup frozen or fresh green peas

Squeeze of fresh lime or lemon juice (optional)

Chopped fresh parsley, for garnish

As much as I adore the classic, dill-flecked Jewish chicken soup I grew up with, it's this Lebanese version that I find myself craving as soon as the weather turns chilly and damp. Simmered with cinnamon, cardamom, and allspice, it's a richer, spicier version that still has a homey, familiar appeal. It's made with both rice and skinny noodles, which is a boon for people who can never choose between chicken rice soup and chicken noodle soup. Here you get both and, even better, the noodles have been toasted in butter until golden brown before being added to the soup pot. And a squeeze of lime and handful of peas stirred in right at the end add both color and tang. Don't let the long list of ingredients deter you; it's what makes this such an excellent, complex soup.

---

1. Using the sauté function, melt the butter in the pressure cooker pot. Add the onion and shallot and cook, stirring occasionally, until translucent, about 5 minutes. Add the noodles and cook, stirring frequently, until golden, about 6 minutes. Transfer to a bowl and set aside. Do not wipe out the pressure cooker pot.

2. Using the sauté function, toast the cinnamon, salt, pepper, allspice, cardamom, cumin, and nutmeg in the pressure cooker for 30 seconds. Tie kitchen twine around the parsley, rosemary, and thyme, then add to the pot along with the carrots, chicken thighs, stock, and 6 cups water. (If you don't have kitchen twine, just throw the herbs into the pot; you can fish them out later with a slotted spoon.)

3. Lock the lid into place and cook on high pressure for 8 minutes. Let the pressure release naturally for 10 minutes, then drape a kitchen towel over the vent and manually release the remaining pressure. (This prevents the brothy steam from splattering everywhere.)

4. Remove and discard the herbs and cinnamon stick, and transfer the chicken to a cutting board to cool.

5. Stir in the rice. Lock the lid into place and cook on high pressure for 1 minute. Let the pressure release naturally for 10 minutes, then drape a kitchen towel over the vent and manually release the remaining pressure.

6. Meanwhile, shred or cut the chicken into bite-size pieces.

7. When the rice has finished cooking, stir in the shredded chicken, noodle/onion mixture, and peas. Using the sauté function, simmer the contents for 1 to 3 minutes to meld the flavors and cook the peas. Spoon into serving bowls and top with a squeeze of lime, if desired, and chopped parsley.

COOK IT SLOW

Sauté the ingredients in step 1 and set aside. Add all the ingredients in step 2, along with the rice from step 5. Slow cook on high for 4 to 6 hours or low for 7 to 9 hours. In the last 10 minutes of cooking, remove the herb bunch and transfer the chicken to a cutting board to rest. Shred the chicken and stir into the soup along with the reserved noodle/onion mixture. Cook for 10 minutes longer on high. Serve.

COD + POTATO CHOWDER

ACTIVE TIME: 20 MINUTES
PRESSURE COOK TIME: 4 MINUTES
TOTAL TIME: 50 MINUTES
YIELD: 4 TO 6 SERVINGS

---

2 ounces bacon (optional), diced

2 tablespoons unsalted butter

1 large onion, diced

1 fennel bulb (or use 2 celery stalks), trimmed and diced

1 teaspoon kosher salt

¼ cup dry (white) vermouth or white wine

1 large russet or Yukon Gold potato, peeled and cut into ¾-inch cubes

1 quart purchased fish stock, or vegetable broth, preferably homemade (page 109)

2 sprigs fresh thyme

1 pound cod or other white, flaky fish, cut into bite-size pieces

¼ cup heavy cream or whole milk

Fennel fronds, or chopped chives or parsley, for garnish

Substituting fennel for the usual celery gives this chowder a gentle licorice note that—along with a splash of herbal vermouth—makes for an especially complex soup. If you can't find good, sustainably caught cod, choose another white flaky fish such as hake or porgy. And if you want to add color and sweetness to your bowl, stir a cup of fresh or frozen corn kernels into the pot along with the fish.

---

1. If using bacon, set the pressure cooker to sauté and cook the bacon, stirring occasionally, until golden, about 5 minutes. Using a slotted spoon, scoop out the bacon and transfer it to a plate lined with paper towels and set aside. Drain the bacon fat from the pot (either reserve for another use or discard).

2. Using the sauté function, melt the butter in the pot, then stir in the onion, fennel, and ½ teaspoon of the salt. Cook, stirring occasionally, until the vegetables are soft and translucent, about 7 minutes. Add the vermouth and let simmer until it reduces to a thin glaze, about 3 minutes. Stir in the potato, fish stock, and thyme.

3. Lock the lid into place and cook on high pressure for 3 minutes. Let the pressure release naturally for 5 minutes, then drape a kitchen towel over the vent and manually release the remaining pressure. (This prevents the brothy steam from splattering everywhere.)

4. Moving quickly, so as to keep the heat in the pressure cooker pot, add the cod to the pot along with the remaining ½ teaspoon salt.

5. Lock the lid back in place and cook on low pressure for 1 minute. Let the pressure release naturally for 5 minutes, then drape a kitchen towel over the vent and manually release the rest of the pressure.

6. Add the bacon back to the pot and gently stir in the cream or milk. Adjust the seasoning if needed. Spoon the chowder into serving bowls and garnish with the herbs. Serve hot.

CHICKEN + RICE SOUP WITH FETA + DILL

ACTIVE TIME: 5 MINUTES

PRESSURE COOK TIME: 9 MINUTES

TOTAL TIME: 40 MINUTES

YIELD: 6 TO 8 SERVINGS

This zesty soup—a more complex take on the classic chicken soup with rice—is bright with lemon, fragrant with nutmeg and dill, and both salty and creamy from a topping of crumbled feta cheese. Even better, it's fast, satisfying, and even freezes well, though don't add the feta until right before serving.

2 quarts chicken stock, preferably homemade (page 108)

4 boneless, skinless chicken thighs

¼ teaspoon freshly grated nutmeg

Long strips of zest from 1 lemon

1 bay leaf

¾ cup short-grain white rice

½ teaspoon kosher salt, plus more if needed

¼ cup fresh lemon juice, plus more if needed

⅓ cup fresh dill, finely chopped

½ cup crumbled feta cheese, for serving

1. In the pressure cooker pot, combine the stock, 2 cups water, the chicken thighs, and nutmeg. Tie together the lemon zest and bay leaf with kitchen twine if you like, and drop the bundle in (or just drop the zest and bay leaf in without tying; you can fish them out later).

2. Lock the lid into place and cook on high pressure for 8 minutes. Drape a kitchen towel over the vent and manually release the pressure. (This prevents the brothy steam from splattering everywhere.)

3. Transfer the chicken thighs to a plate. Let them cool, then shred the meat.

4. Meanwhile, in the pressure cooker pot, stir in the rice and salt. Lock the lid into place and cook on high pressure for 1 minute. Let the pressure release naturally for 10 minutes, then drape a kitchen towel over the vent and manually release the remaining pressure.

5. Remove the lemon zest and bay leaf from the soup. Stir in the lemon juice and dill. Taste and add more lemon and/or salt if needed. Add the shredded chicken to the pot. To serve, ladle the soup into bowls and top with feta.

COOK IT SLOW

Add all the ingredients (except the lemon juice, dill, and feta) to the slow cooker. Cook on high for 5 hours or low for 8 hours. In the last 10 minutes of cooking, remove the chicken thighs and shred the meat. Check the rice: If it is not done, cover and let sit for another 10 to 15 minutes. Proceed with step 5.

CONGEE WITH CHICKEN (RICE PORRIDGE)

ACTIVE TIME: 15 MINUTES
PRESSURE COOK TIME: 20 MINUTES
TOTAL TIME: 55 MINUTES
YIELD: 4 TO 6 SERVINGS

---

2 tablespoons toasted sesame oil, plus more for drizzling

3 fat garlic cloves, thinly sliced

Kosher salt

3 scallions, thinly sliced, white and green parts kept separate

1-inch piece fresh ginger, peeled and smashed

1 cup short-grain white rice

2 quarts chicken stock, preferably homemade (page 108), or water

1 pound bone-in, skin-on chicken thighs

Chopped fresh cilantro, for serving

Soy sauce, for serving

COOK IT SLOW

After step 2, slow cook on high for 5 to 6 hours or low for 8 to 10 hours.

This thick rice porridge is classic comfort food in many parts of China. The traditional cooking method calls for simmering the rice and broth for hours and hours, but a pressure cooker can cut that time down to a mere 20 minutes. If you don't want to bother with the fried garlic slices, skip the first step and instead sauté the garlic with the ginger and scallions and leave it in the pot when you cook the rice.

---

1. Using the sauté function (on low, if possible), heat the sesame oil, garlic, and a pinch of salt in the pressure cooker pot. Cook, stirring frequently, until the garlic is light golden, 4 to 6 minutes. Transfer with a slotted spoon to a plate lined with paper towels and set aside. Leave the oil in the pot.

2. Stir in the scallion whites (save the greens for garnish), ginger, and another pinch of salt and cook until the scallions are soft, about 2 minutes. Stir in the rice, stock, and 1 teaspoon salt. Top with the chicken.

3. Lock the lid into place and cook on high pressure for 20 minutes. Let the pressure release naturally.

4. Transfer the chicken to a cutting board to cool. Remove the skin, then shred the chicken and skin, if you like (or discard the skin). Return the chicken to the pot and mix into the rice. Taste and add more salt if needed (remember that you will be topping this with soy sauce, so don't overdo it).

5. To serve, ladle the congee into bowls and top with the fried garlic, scallion greens, cilantro, and a drizzle of soy sauce and sesame oil.

BEEF PHO WITH RICE NOODLES + BASIL

ACTIVE TIME: 20 MINUTES
PRESSURE COOK TIME: 20 MINUTES
TOTAL TIME: 1 HOUR 15 MINUTES
YIELD: 4 SERVINGS

[illegible] star anise pods

1 cinnamon stick

3 whole cloves

2-inch piece fresh ginger, peeled and sliced

6 scallions, white and green parts kept separate

2 quarts beef stock or bone broth, preferably homemade (see page 108)

2 quarts chicken stock, preferably homemade (see page 108)

1 teaspoon fine sea salt

10 ounces dried rice noodles, preferably flat ones

8 to 10 ounces eye round or sirloin steak, thinly sliced, at room temperature

2 to 4 tablespoons Asian fish sauce, to taste

2 teaspoons sugar, or to taste

Basil leaves, preferably Vietnamese or Thai, for serving

Bean sprouts, for serving

Lime wedges, for serving

Thinly sliced jalapeño chile, for serving

In a traditional Vietnamese pho, dense cuts of beef and bones are simmered for hours into a fragrant broth rich with aromatics including star anise, cinnamon, cloves, and ginger. For serving, the tender meat is sliced and added back to the broth, along with rice noodles and a whole host of garnishes—herbs, bean sprouts, and tangy fresh lime. It's a hearty, warming soup that's also fresh and crunchy.

This simplified version calls for premade broth that's briefly pressure-cooked with the aromatics—a quicker way to add their flavor. And instead of the long-simmered beef, thin slices of raw steak are added to the hot broth, which cooks it on contact (raw steak is sometimes added to traditional pho, too, along with the stewed beef).

Make sure to slice the beef very thinly and to have the broth piping hot when the two meet; otherwise, the steak might not cook properly. Freezing the meat for an hour or so before slicing helps you get extra-thin slivers. Or, ask your butcher to slice it for you.

---

1. Using the sauté function, toast the star anise, cinnamon stick, and cloves in the pressure cooker pot until fragrant, 1 to 2 minutes (you don't need oil for this). Stir in the ginger and scallion whites and cook for another 1 minute. Pour in the beef stock, chicken stock, and salt.

2. Lock the lid into place and cook on high pressure for 20 minutes. Let the pressure release naturally for 10 minutes, then drape a kitchen towel over the vent and manually release the remaining pressure. (This prevents the brothy steam from splattering everywhere.)

3. Meanwhile, place the noodles in a large bowl. Cover with very hot water and let them sit until soft and pliable, 3 to 5 minutes. Drain the noodles, then divide them among serving bowls and top with the thinly sliced raw beef.

4. Once finished cooking, strain the stock and return it to the pressure cooker pot (or you can use a slotted spoon to scoop out the solids from the broth).

5. Using the sauté function, bring the stock to a boil. Stir in the fish sauce and sugar, then taste and adjust the seasoning if needed—the broth should have a good balance of sweet and salty; the acid will come from the lime juice.

6. Ladle the piping hot broth over the beef and noodles. Serve with chopped scallion greens, basil, bean sprouts, lime wedges, and jalapeño.

COOK IT SLOW

After step 1, cook the stock on high for 4 to 6 hours or low for 8 to 10 hours. Prep the noodles and beef as described in step 3. Proceed with steps 4 through 6.

COMFORTING SIDES

ZESTY BRUSSELS SPROUTS WITH PANCETTA

ACTIVE TIME: 10 MINUTES
PRESSURE COOK TIME: 2 MINUTES
TOTAL TIME: 20 MINUTES
YIELD: 4 TO 6 SERVINGS

---

1 tablespoon extra-virgin olive oil

2 ounces pancetta or bacon, cut into ¼-inch dice

1 pound Brussels sprouts, trimmed and halved

2 teaspoons Asian fish sauce

½ tablespoon Sriracha

1 teaspoon honey

1 lime, zest grated and halved

Spicy, porky, and very tender, these Brussels sprouts will perk up even the simplest of meals. I especially like them as an accompaniment to roasted chicken, fish, or grilled steak. Or, turn them into a simple grain bowl by piling the sprouts on top of brown rice or quinoa, along with some sliced radishes and their greens, and sesame seeds for crunch. A fried egg on top wouldn't be out of place, either.

---

1. Using the sauté function (set on low, if possible), heat the oil and pancetta in the pressure cooker pot and cook until golden, about 2 minutes.

2. Add the Brussels sprouts, fish sauce, Sriracha, honey, lime zest, and the juice of half the lime. Toss to coat.

3. Lock the lid into place and cook on high pressure for 2 minutes. Manually release the pressure.

4. Using the sauté function (set on high, if possible), cook the sprouts, tossing gently, until the liquid in the pot thickens to a glaze, 1 to 2 minutes. Serve hot or warm.

TURKISH BULGUR PILAF WITH PISTACHIOS + CURRANTS

ACTIVE TIME: 10 MINUTES
PRESSURE COOK TIME: 10 MINUTES
TOTAL TIME: 35 MINUTES
YIELD: [illegible] TO [illegible] SERVINGS

---

4 tablespoons unsalted butter

3 scallions, thinly sliced, white and green parts kept separate

1 cup medium-grain bulgur

¾ teaspoon kosher salt, plus more if needed

¼ teaspoon ground turmeric

⅛ teaspoon ground cardamom

⅛ teaspoon ground cinnamon

2 cups vegetable broth or chicken stock, preferably homemade (page 108)

¼ cup dried currants

½ teaspoon finely grated orange zest

Pinch of Turkish pepper or cayenne

⅓ cup pistachios, toasted and chopped

Drizzling spiced, orange zest–flecked brown butter over bulgur pilaf elevates a simple side dish into a spectacular one, especially when you've also got currants and toasted pistachios added to the mix. You can use this recipe as a template for your own fruit and nut combinations: sliced almonds and dried cherries, toasted pecans and chopped dried apricots, golden raisins and cashews. Use whatever you love and you can't go wrong.

---

1. Using the sauté function, melt 1 tablespoon of the butter in the pressure cooker pot. Stir in the scallion whites and cook until softened, about 2 minutes. Stir in the bulgur and salt and cook until nutty and toasted, about another 2 minutes.

2. Stir in the turmeric, cardamom, and cinnamon until combined, then stir in the broth.

3. Lock the lid into place and cook on low pressure for 10 minutes. Manually release the pressure. Stir the bulgur, then cover the pot with the lid (but don't lock it on) and let it sit for 5 minutes.

4. While the bulgur is cooking, in a small bowl, cover the currants with boiling water and let them soak until soft, about 5 minutes. Drain.

5. In a small pot on the stove, combine the remaining 3 tablespoons butter, the orange zest, and Turkish pepper and heat over medium heat until the butter browns, about 3 minutes. Remove from the heat.

6. After the bulgur has sat for 5 minutes, remove the cover from the pot and fold in the brown butter, drained currants, pistachios, and scallion greens. Taste and add more salt if needed. Serve while warm.

CURRIED COLLARD GREENS

ACTIVE TIME: 10 MINUTES
PRESSURE COOK TIME: 4 MINUTES
TOTAL TIME: 20 MINUTES
YIELD: 4 SERVINGS

---

1 tablespoon coconut oil, sunflower oil, or canola oil

1 small onion, diced

2 garlic cloves, minced

1 teaspoon curry powder

1 tablespoon tomato paste

Pinch of cayenne pepper

½ cup vegetable broth or chicken stock, preferably homemade (page 108), or water

8 cups sliced collard greens (1 to 2 bunches sliced into 1-inch-wide ribbons, see headnote)

¼ teaspoon fine sea salt, plus more if needed

1 teaspoon fresh lime juice, plus more if needed

When simmered on the stove, thick and leathery collard greens can take upwards of half an hour to turn silky and lush. The pressure cooker does them beautifully in under 5 minutes. In addition to being a deeply savory side dish, these tender greens also make an unusual vegetarian main dish for 2 when served over quinoa or tofu noodles for added protein.

The easiest way to slice the collard greens is to take out the ribs, then stack 4 or 5 leaves on top of one another. Roll the leaves into a cylinder and cut crosswise into 1-inch-wide ribbons.

---

1. Using the sauté function, heat the oil in the pressure cooker pot. Add the onion and garlic and sauté until the onion is translucent, 2 to 4 minutes. Add the curry powder and sauté for 20 seconds, then stir in the tomato paste and cayenne and sauté for 1 minute longer.

2. Add the broth to the pot and let simmer for 2 minutes to reduce it slightly. Add the collard greens and salt.

3. Lock the lid into place and cook on high pressure for 4 minutes. Manually release the pressure.

4. Stir the lime juice into the pot, then taste and add more lime juice and salt if needed. Transfer to a dish to serve.

COOK IT SLOW

After steps 1 and 2, cook on high for 1 to 2 hours or low for 3 to 4 hours.

SPICY SWEET POTATO PUREE (OR CASSEROLE) WITH COCONUT

ACTIVE TIME: 10 MINUTES
PRESSURE COOK TIME: 4 MINUTES
TOTAL TIME: 30 MINUTES (IF NOT BAKING)
YIELD: 3 TO 4 SERVINGS

---

2 pounds sweet potatoes, peeled and diced

1 14-ounce can full-fat coconut milk

1 tablespoon light brown sugar, or more to taste

½ teaspoon kosher salt, or more to taste

½ teaspoon finely grated orange zest

¼ teaspoon ground cinnamon, or more to taste

¼ teaspoon ground cardamom, or more to taste

⅛ teaspoon cayenne pepper

2 large eggs (for casserole)

1 cup sweetened shredded coconut (for casserole)

Diced sweet potatoes cook in minutes under pressure and make a velvety and unusual vegetable dish when spiced with cinnamon, cardamom, and cayenne and pureed with coconut milk. You can serve this either as a silky, slightly runny puree, or mix it with eggs, top with coconut, and bake it into a fluffy, crunchy-topped casserole. One recipe, two excellent serving options.

---

1. In the pressure cooker pot, combine the sweet potatoes, coconut milk, brown sugar, salt, orange zest, cinnamon, cardamom, and cayenne.

2. Lock the lid into place and cook on high pressure for 4 minutes. Manually release the pressure.

3. For a creamy puree: With an immersion blender, puree the potatoes until smooth and creamy (or transfer the mixture to a food processor). Taste and adjust the seasoning if necessary. Serve while warm.

4. For a crunchy-topped casserole: Preheat the oven to 400°F. Beat the eggs into the cooked potato mixture, then scrape the mixture into a 9 x 9-inch baking dish, and sprinkle the shredded coconut on top. Bake until the top is golden, about 20 minutes.

COCONUT RICE

ACTIVE TIME: 5 MINUTES
PRESSURE COOK TIME: 5 MINUTES
TOTAL TIME: 35 MINUTES
YIELD: 4 SERVINGS

1 tablespoon coconut oil

1½ cups short-grain white rice

1¼ cups full-fat coconut milk

¼ teaspoon kosher salt

Lightly sweet and very creamy, coconut rice is exactly right when you want something on the decadent end of the side dish spectrum.

1. Using the sauté function (set on high, if possible), melt the coconut oil. In the pressure cooker pot, add the rice and cook for 2 minutes to toast. Stir in the coconut milk and salt.

2. Lock the lid into place and cook on high pressure for 3 to 5 minutes. Let the pressure release naturally for 10 minutes, then manually release the remaining pressure.

3. As soon as the pressure has released, remove the cover and fluff the rice with a fork. Place a kitchen towel over the pressure cooker pot, replace the lid (but don't lock it on), and let it sit for 10 minutes. Fluff again and serve.

MIDDLE EASTERN RICE + VERMICELLI PILAF

ACTIVE TIME: 10 MINUTES
PRESSURE COOK TIME: 8 MINUTES
TOTAL TIME: 30 MINUTES
YIELD: 3 TO 4 SERVINGS

3 tablespoons unsalted butter

½ cup vermicelli or angel hair noodles (break them up with your hands so they fit into a measuring cup)

2 cups long-grain white rice, unrinsed

1½ teaspoons kosher salt

1 quart chicken stock or vegetable broth, preferably homemade (page 108)

1 cinnamon stick

Chopped parsley or mint, for serving (optional)

Sliced almonds, for serving (optional)

Flaky sea salt, for serving (optional)

Traditional Mediterranean pilafs often combine rice and thin little noodles, both of which are browned in butter before being simmered in stock. This one, perfumed with a cinnamon stick added to the broth, is a nice change from the usual.

As a variation, a sprinkling of toasted pine nuts or slivered almonds would make a great garnish here, adding a nutty crunch.

1. Using the sauté function, melt the butter in the pressure cooker pot. Add the pasta and cook, stirring frequently, until golden brown, 2 to 3 minutes.

2. Add the rice and salt and cook, stirring frequently, for 2 minutes. Stir in the stock, cinnamon stick, and ¾ cup water.

3. Lock the lid into place and cook on high pressure for 8 minutes. Let the pressure release naturally.

4. As soon as the pressure has released, quickly remove the cover and fluff the rice with a fork. Place a kitchen towel over the pressure cooker pot, replace the lid (but don't lock it on), and let it sit for 10 minutes. Remove the cinnamon stick. Fluff the rice again and serve with parsley or mint and sliced almonds and flaky sea salt, if desired.

HERBED BABY POTATOES

ACTIVE TIME: 15 MINUTES
PRESSURE COOK TIME: 7 MINUTES
TOTAL TIME: 30 MINUTES
YIELD: 2 TO 4 SERVINGS

---

1 tablespoon unsalted butter

3 tablespoons extra-virgin olive oil

1½ pounds new or baby potatoes (about 1¼ inches in diameter), scrubbed and pricked with a fork

Kosher salt

½ tablespoon fresh rosemary needles, minced

2 garlic cloves, minced

½ cup vegetable broth or chicken stock, preferably homemade (page 108), or water

---

In this richly flavored side dish, small potatoes get browned in a mix of butter and oil, then pressure-cooked with rosemary, garlic, and broth until very tender and imbued with aromatics. The timing here works with potatoes that are about 1¼ inches in diameter. If yours are smaller, take the cooking time down by a minute or two; or cut larger potatoes into pieces.

---

1. Using the sauté function, heat the butter and oil in the pressure cooker pot. Stir in the potatoes and ½ teaspoon salt and cook, stirring occasionally, until golden brown, about 12 minutes.

2. Stir in the rosemary and garlic and cook for another 30 seconds. Then stir in the broth.

3. Lock the lid into place and cook on high pressure for 7 minutes. Let the pressure release naturally for 10 minutes, then manually release the remaining pressure.

4. Scoop the potatoes out with a slotted spoon and transfer them to a plate. Sprinkle with salt to taste. Serve warm.

1/4 CUP = 4 TBS

SWEET COMFORTS

LEMON-VANILLA RICE PUDDING WITH WHIPPED CREAM

ACTIVE TIME: 10 MINUTES
PRESSURE COOK TIME: 4 MINUTES
TOTAL TIME: 30 MINUTES, PLUS 4 HOURS CHILLING
YIELD: 4 TO 6 SERVINGS

⅔ cup Arborio or other short-grain white rice

3 cups whole milk

⅓ cup sugar

1 cinnamon stick

1 teaspoon finely grated lemon zest

Pinch of kosher salt

½ vanilla bean, halved lengthwise

¾ cup heavy cream

2 egg yolks

½ cup raisins (optional)

Ground cinnamon, for serving (optional)

Whipped cream, for serving (optional)

Using a vanilla bean makes this creamy pudding extra special and aromatic. But if you don't have one on hand, just stir 1 tablespoon vanilla extract into the pudding along with the egg yolks. Although rice pudding is traditionally served cold, I also like this when it's still warm and a little runny, poured over sliced strawberries and raspberries, which add both juiciness and acidity.

---

1. In the pressure cooker pot, stir together the rice, milk, sugar, cinnamon stick, lemon zest, and salt. Use the tip of a paring knife to scrape the vanilla seeds out of the pod into the pot and add the vanilla bean, too.

2. Lock the lid into place and cook on high pressure for 4 minutes. Let the pressure release naturally for 10 minutes, then manually release the remaining pressure.

3. Remove and discard the cinnamon stick and vanilla bean.

4. In a small bowl, whisk together the cream and yolks. Whisk into the rice, continuing to stir until thickened, 2 to 4 minutes. The residual heat of the rice will cook the yolks. Stir in the raisins (if using).

5. Spoon the pudding into serving bowls, then cover with plastic wrap and chill for at least 4 hours. The pudding will thicken as it cools. Serve with a sprinkle of ground cinnamon and whipped cream, if desired.

GINGER-LEMON CHEESECAKE

ACTIVE TIME: 25 MINUTES
PRESSURE COOK TIME: 36 MINUTES
TOTAL TIME: 1 HOUR 15 MINUTES, PLUS 8 HOURS CHILLING
YIELD: 6 SERVINGS

FOR THE CRUST

1 cup (153 grams) ginger snap or ginger wafer cookie crumbs (do not use cream-filled ginger cookies)

3½ tablespoons unsalted butter, melted

1 tablespoon light brown sugar

⅛ teaspoon fine sea salt

FOR THE FILLING

12 ounces cream cheese, thoroughly softened

½ cup packed light brown sugar

⅔ cup full-fat sour cream

2 tablespoons Grand Marnier

1½ teaspoons finely grated lemon zest

Pinch of salt

3 large eggs, at room temperature

6 tablespoons chopped candied ginger

With a ginger cookie crust and plenty of lemon and candied ginger in its velvety filling, this cheesecake is livelier and more complex than the usual recipe. As with any kind of cheesecake, you'll need to plan ahead. Not only does the cream cheese need to be softened for a few hours ahead at room temperature (or you could pop it in the microwave), the finished cheesecake also needs to chill for at least 8 hours.

1. Preheat the oven to [illegible].

2. Make the crust: In a small bowl, combine the cookie crumbs, melted butter, brown sugar, and salt. Pat the mixture evenly into the bottom and most of the way up the sides of a 7-inch springform pan. Bake until the crust has set and is golden brown, 8 to 12 minutes. Transfer to a rack to cool completely.

3. Make the filling: Using an electric mixer fitted with the paddle attachment, beat the cream cheese and brown sugar until very smooth. This could take several minutes if your cream cheese is not thoroughly soft. Add the sour cream, Grand Marnier, 1 teaspoon of the lemon zest, and salt and beat again at medium speed until all the ingredients are incorporated. On medium-low speed, beat in the eggs, one at a time, scraping down the sides of the bowl after each addition. Beat in 3 tablespoons of the candied ginger. Pour the filling into the crust and cover with foil.

4. Pour 1½ cups water into the pressure cooker pot. If your steamer rack has handles, place the pan on the rack and lower everything into the pressure cooker pot. If your rack does not have handles, first place the rack in the pot, then lower in the pan using a homemade sling (see page 17).

5. Lock the lid into place and cook on high pressure for 36 minutes. Let the pressure release naturally.

6. Transfer the cheesecake to a rack, remove the foil, and allow the cake to cool completely. Cover and chill for at least 8 hours. Just before serving, mix together the remaining ½ teaspoon of lemon zest and 3 tablespoons of candied ginger, and sprinkle on top of the cheesecake.

JAPANESE CHEESECAKE

ACTIVE TIME: 25 MINUTES
PRESSURE COOK TIME: 17 MINUTES
TOTAL TIME: 1½ HOURS, PLUS 1 HOUR [illegible] TIME
YIELD: 8 SERVINGS

---

3 large eggs, separated

½ cup granulated sugar

2 teaspoons finely grated lemon zest

5 ounces cream cheese, thoroughly softened

¼ cup whole milk

½ cup cake flour

¼ cup cornstarch

1 teaspoon unsweetened cocoa powder (optional)

1 teaspoon confectioners' sugar (optional)

Sliced strawberries or other berries (optional)

Lighter and fluffier than a New York cheesecake, this mousse-like confection melts in the mouth. It takes a lot of beating in many separate bowls to get the right texture, but it's worth it. (Having a second bowl that fits into your electric mixer helps.) The cocoa powder/confectioners' sugar topping does double duty: It adds a bitter note to the cake, which I like against the sweet fluffy filling, and it hides the rather unattractively pale top of the cake. Sliced strawberries or other berries would also work as a topping, so feel free to substitute them for the cocoa powder and confectioners' sugar.

Note that your cream cheese must be softened before you start beating. Otherwise, you'll likely end up with lumps in your batter. Stick your cream cheese in the microwave for 20 to 60 seconds if it is cold.

---

1. Line the bottom of a 7-inch springform pan with a round of parchment paper. (Do not grease the pan, which would inhibit the cake from rising as much.)

2. Using an electric mixer fitted with the whisk attachment, beat the egg yolks and ¼ cup of the sugar on medium-high until pale and thick, 3 to 5 minutes.

3. In a large bowl, using a handheld electric mixer or a whisk and a lot of muscle power, mix the lemon zest into the softened cream cheese until smooth and free of lumps, constantly scraping down the sides of the bowl. Slowly mix in the milk until the mixture is completely smooth.

4. Gently fold the yolk mixture into the cream cheese mixture.

5. In a clean, dry bowl of an electric mixer fitted with a clean whisk attachment, whip the egg whites on high for 1 minute. Reduce the speed to medium-high and add the remaining ¼ cup sugar, 1 tablespoon at a time, whipping for a minute after each addition until the egg whites form soft peaks.

6. In a medium bowl, whisk together the cake flour and cornstarch. Sift the cake flour mixture over the cream cheese mixture and gently fold the two until they are almost combined. The batter will thicken considerably.

7. Adding one-third of the egg whites at a time, fold them into the batter until just combined. Scrape the batter into the prepared springform pan and smooth the top into an even layer.

8. Pour about 1 inch of water into the pressure cooker pot. If your steamer rack has handles, place the pan on the rack and lower everything into the pressure cooker pot. If your rack does not have handles, first place the rack in the pot, then lower in the pan using a homemade sling (see page 17).

9. Lock the lid into place and cook on high pressure for 17 minutes. Let the pressure release naturally for 10 minutes, then manually release the remaining pressure. The cake should be slightly domed and jiggly but not wet looking.

10. Allow the cake to cool on a rack at room temperature for at least 1 hour or up to 6 hours. For longer storage, chill in the fridge.

11. Just before serving, in a small bowl, whisk together the cocoa powder and confectioners' sugar (if using). Use a small sieve to dust the cocoa-sugar mixture over the cake. Alternatively, top the cake with berries.

FLOURLESS CHOCOLATE TRUFFLE CAKE

ACTIVE TIME: 10 MINUTES
PRESSURE COOK TIME: 30 MINUTES
TOTAL TIME: 50 MINUTES, PLUS 6 HOURS CHILLING
YIELD: 6 TO 8 SERVINGS

---

2 sticks (8 ounces) unsalted butter, plus more for the pan

1 pound bittersweet chocolate, coarsely chopped (or use chips)

¼ teaspoon fine sea salt

1 teaspoon vanilla extract

6 large eggs

Confectioners' sugar, for serving

This is the fudgiest, richest thing I've ever made in my electric pressure cooker, perfect for when nothing short of chocolate decadence will do. The only sugar in this recipe comes from the chocolate itself, so you can make this a bit sweeter by using semisweet chocolate instead of bittersweet, or dial back the sweetness by using an extra bittersweet chocolate. I like chocolate in a range of 60% to 64% cacao here, but feel free to go up to 74% for something very dark and bitter.

---

1. Line the bottom of a 7-inch springform pan with a round of parchment paper. Butter the parchment and the sides of the pan.

2. In a microwave-safe medium bowl, combine the butter and chocolate. Microwave the mixture in 30-second intervals, stirring after each, until the chocolate is almost melted. Remove the bowl from the microwave and continue stirring until the chocolate is completely melted, about 1 minute. (This can also be done in a double boiler on the stove.) Stir in the salt and vanilla.

3. Using an electric mixer fitted with the whisk, beat the eggs until they turn pale and frothy and double in size, 2 to 3 minutes (or use a whisk to beat the eggs by hand, though be prepared for a good 5 to 7 minutes of beating). Then whisk a small amount of the warm chocolate mixture into the eggs. This allows the eggs to temper so that they do not curdle. Slowly add the rest of the chocolate to the bowl, whisking constantly. The batter will thicken considerably. Pour the batter in the prepared pan and smooth the top with a spatula. Cover the pan with aluminum foil.

4. Pour 1 cup water into the pressure cooker pot. If your steamer rack has handles, place the pan on the rack and lower everything into the pressure cooker pot. If your rack does not have handles, first place the rack in the pot, then lower in the pan using a homemade sling (see page 17).

5. Lock the lid into place and cook on high pressure for 30 minutes. Let the pressure release naturally.

6. Remove the pan from the pot and let cool for 15 minutes at room temperature (keep the foil on). Then transfer the pan to the fridge to chill completely, at least 6 hours. Once chilled, run a butter knife around the inside of the pan, then unmold the cake. Just before serving, dust with confectioners' sugar.

BITTERSWEET CHOCOLATE FLANS

ACTIVE TIME: 15 MINUTES
PRESSURE COOK TIME: 6 MINUTES
TOTAL TIME: 45 MINUTES, PLUS 4 HOURS CHILLING
YIELD: 6 SERVINGS

¾ cup plus ⅓ cup granulated sugar

4 ounces bittersweet (preferably 66% to 74% cacao) chocolate, chopped (or use chips)

1 cup whole milk

½ cup heavy cream

3 large eggs

1 teaspoon vanilla extract

Pinch of kosher salt

Crème fraîche or sour cream, for serving (optional)

What could be better than chocolate pudding? How about chocolate pudding coated in a syrupy amber caramel, as it is here in this silky flan? It's worth seeking out good bittersweet chocolate for this recipe, rather than the usual semisweet. It makes for a more balanced, less sweet dessert. But if you can get only semisweet chocolate, bring down the sugar in the custard by a tablespoon or two. Another thing to note: The darker your caramel, the less sweet it will be, so try to get it good and deeply brown before you take it off the heat.

---

1. Have six 4- to 6-ounce ramekins at the ready near the stove. In a medium saucepan or skillet, combine ¾ cup of the sugar and 2 tablespoons water. Cook over medium-high heat, swirling the pan occasionally but without stirring, until the sugar begins to caramelize, 5 to 8 minutes. Continue to cook until the caramel turns dark amber (the color of an Irish setter; this will happen in another minute or so after the sugar begins to caramelize). Immediately remove the pan from the heat and pour the hot caramel into the ramekins, swirling each one so the caramel reaches partway up the sides of the cup. If the caramel starts to harden before you're finished pouring it out, put the pot back on the stove and reheat briefly until it liquefies.

2. Pour 1 cup water into the pressure cooker pot. Place a steamer rack/trivet in the bottom.

3. Place the chocolate into a blender or food processor bowl and pulse it once or twice to break it up.

4. In a pot on the stove or in the microwave, heat the milk and cream until it just reaches a simmer. Pour it into the blender or food processor with the chocolate and let sit until the mixture cools slightly and the chocolate melts, about 5 minutes.

5. Briefly blend the mixture, then add the eggs, remaining 1/3 cup sugar, the vanilla, and salt and pulse until smooth.

6. Pour the chocolate mixture into the ramekins, cover each with a piece of aluminum foil, and place three ramekins on top of the trivet. Stack the remaining three on top of the other ramekins, staggering them (you will have two layers of ramekins).

7. Lock the lid into place and cook on low pressure for 6 minutes. Let the pressure release naturally for 10 minutes, then manually release the remaining pressure.

8. Use tongs to transfer the ramekins to a baking sheet, tray, or plate. Remove the foil and let the flans cool to room temperature. Cover the flans with plastic wrap and transfer them to the refrigerator to chill until firm, at least 4 hours. They will keep in the refrigerator for up to 5 days.

9. To serve, run a thin spatula or butter knife around the edge of each ramekin and invert the flans onto serving plates. Serve with crème fraîche, if you like.

CHOCOLATE-BOURBON LAVA CAKES WITH SEA SALT

ACTIVE TIME: 15 MINUTES
PRESSURE COOK TIME: 9 MINUTES
TOTAL TIME: 38 MINUTES
YIELD: 4 INDIVIDUAL CAKES

---

1 stick (4 ounces) unsalted butter, plus more for the ramekins

6 ounces bittersweet (65% to 74% cacao) chocolate, chopped (or use chips)

¾ cup confectioners' sugar

⅛ teaspoon fine sea salt

3 large eggs

1 egg yolk

1 tablespoon bourbon or vanilla extract

6 tablespoons all-purpose flour

Flaky sea salt, for serving

Crème fraîche, sour cream, or ice cream, for serving

If you love to bake, you probably have all the necessary ingredients for this incredibly simple recipe already stocked in your pantry. Which means you can whip up these runny-centered, fudgey cakes whenever the urge for something bittersweet and gooey hits. Note that the higher the percentage of cacao in your chocolate, the less sweet the dessert will be. I like to use bittersweet chocolate that's between 65% and 74%, which to me is the right balance of cocoa solids and sugar. If you've got only semisweet chocolate on hand (usually around 45% to 55%), you can reduce the confectioners' sugar by a few tablespoons to compensate.

---

1. In a microwave-safe medium bowl, melt the butter with the chocolate (or do this in a small saucepan over low heat). Meanwhile, butter four 6-ounce ramekins.

2. To the bowl with the butter/chocolate mixture, add the confectioners' sugar and salt and whisk until cool to the touch. Whisk in the whole eggs and egg yolk, followed by the bourbon and flour. Distribute the mixture evenly among the four ramekins. Cover each with aluminum foil.

3. Pour 1 cup water into the pressure cooker pot. Place a steamer rack/trivet at the bottom of the pot. Stack the ramekins on the rack. You should be able to fit three on the bottom with the fourth placed on top in the center.

4. Lock the lid into place and cook on high pressure for 9 minutes. Manually release the pressure.

5. With tongs, remove the ramekins from the pot and allow them to sit for 3 minutes, still covered with foil. Then remove the foil and run a knife around the edge of each cake. Flip each cake onto a serving plate. Sprinkle with sea salt and top with crème fraîche or ice cream, if you like. Serve immediately.

STICKY TOFFEE PUDDINGS

ACTIVE TIME: [illegible] MINUTES
STEAM COOK TIME: 25 MINUTES
TOTAL TIME: 55 MINUTES
YIELD: 6 SERVINGS

FOR THE CAKES

4 ounces pitted dates, finely chopped (about 1 cup)

1 teaspoon finely grated orange zest

¾ teaspoon baking soda

½ cup boiling water

¼ cup fresh orange juice

1¼ cups all-purpose flour

⅛ teaspoon sea salt

4 tablespoons (½ stick) unsalted butter, at room temperature, plus more for the ramekins

2 tablespoons molasses

1 tablespoon honey

½ cup confectioners' sugar

1 large egg

1 egg yolk

FOR THE SAUCE

1⅓ cups packed light brown sugar

1 cup heavy cream

⅛ teaspoon fine sea salt

1 stick (4 ounces) unsalted butter, cubed

Flaky sea salt, for serving

This is one of my all-time favorite things to have emerged from my multicooker—hot, syrupy little cakes, filled with citrus, molasses, and dates and soaked in a buttery brown-sugar toffee sauce. The key here is to make the sauce on the stove while the cakes steam in the pressure cooker. That way, you can serve the confections while still warm and pleasingly soft in the center. If you manage to have leftovers, store them in the fridge for up to 3 days, then warm them up in the microwave just before serving. They won't be quite as good as when freshly made, but will still be utterly appealing. Note that this recipe uses the steam function on your multicooker, not the pressure function.

---

1. Make the cakes: Pour 2 cups water into the pressure cooker pot. Place a steamer rack/trivet in the bottom. Butter six small (4- to 6-ounce) ramekins.

2. In a heatproof bowl, combine the dates, orange zest, and baking soda. Stir in the boiling water and orange juice and let sit for 10 minutes.

3. Meanwhile, in a medium bowl, whisk together the flour and sea salt.

4. Using an electric mixer, beat together the butter, molasses, honey, and confectioners' sugar. Beat in the whole egg and egg yolk.

5. Beat in half of the date mixture, followed by half of the flour mixture. Repeat, scraping between each addition, until just combined.

6. Scrape into the prepared ramekins, then cover each with aluminum foil. Place three ramekins on the rack, then make a second layer with three more ramekins, staggering them.

7. Lock the lid into place, press the steam button, and steam the cakes for 25 minutes.

8. Meanwhile, make the sauce: In a medium pot, combine the brown sugar, heavy cream, and salt. Bring to a simmer over medium heat, then remove from the heat. Whisk in the butter. (If the sauce separates, use an immersion blender to blend it together.)

9. When the cakes are done, manually release the steam. Use tongs to carefully remove the ramekins from the pressure cooker, and remove the foil. Run a small offset spatula or butter knife around the edges of the ramekins, then invert each cake onto a serving plate.

10. Top the cakes immediately with the sauce, while they are still warm, and sprinkle with sea salt. Serve with more sauce on the side.

CHOCOLATE HAZELNUT CHEESECAKE

ACTIVE TIME: 20 MINUTES
PRESSURE COOK TIME: 32 MINUTES
TOTAL TIME: 1½ HOURS, PLUS 8 HOURS CHILLING
YIELD: 6 SERVINGS

FOR THE CRUST

¾ cup (100 grams) graham cracker crumbs (9 to 11 graham crackers)

3 tablespoons unsalted butter, melted

1 tablespoon dark brown sugar

Pinch of fine sea salt

FOR THE FILLING

16 ounces cream cheese, thoroughly softened

⅓ cup chocolate-hazelnut spread, such as Nutella

2 tablespoons granulated sugar

2 tablespoons heavy cream or whole milk

1 teaspoon vanilla extract

Pinch of fine sea salt

2 large eggs, at room temperature

My favorite way to eat Nutella is to spread it, icing-thick, onto a crusty sourdough baguette. This ultra creamy cheesecake, with its crisp graham cracker crust, is a very close second. If you want to mix things up, you can use shortbread, ginger cookies, snickerdoodles, or inky dark chocolate wafers instead of graham crackers to make the ¾ cup of crumbs. You really can't go wrong.

Note that your cream cheese must be softened before you start beating. Otherwise you'll likely end up with lumps in your batter. Stick your cream cheese in the microwave for 20 to 60 seconds if it is cold.

---

1. Preheat the oven to 350°F.

2. Make the crust: In a small bowl, combine the crumbs, melted butter, brown sugar, and salt. Transfer it to a 7-inch springform pan, patting it all over the bottom and halfway up the sides. Bake until golden brown, 8 to 12 minutes. Transfer to a rack to cool completely.

3. Make the filling: Using an electric mixer fitted with the paddle attachment, beat the cream cheese, chocolate-hazelnut spread, and granulated sugar until very smooth. Beat in the heavy cream, vanilla, and salt. On medium-low speed, beat in the eggs, one at a time, scraping down the sides of the bowl as needed, until fully incorporated.

4. Pour the filling into the crust and cover with foil.

5. Pour 1½ cups water into the pressure cooker. If your steamer rack has handles, place the pan on the rack and lower everything into the pressure cooker pot. If your rack does not have handles, first place the rack in the pot, then lower in the pan using a homemade sling (see page 17).

6. Lock the lid into place and cook on high pressure for 32 minutes. Let the pressure release naturally for 10 minutes, then manually release the remaining pressure.

7. Transfer the cheesecake to a rack, remove the foil, and allow the cake to cool completely. Cover and chill for at least 8 hours before serving.

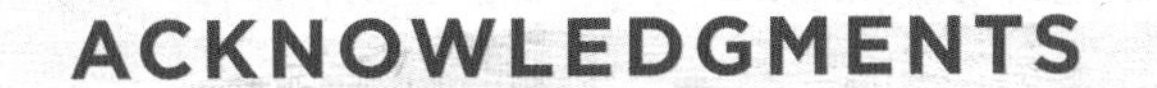

ACKNOWLEDGMENTS

Many thanks to the whole team who helped put together this most comforting of volumes.

First off, I owe my electric pressure cooker obsession to my editors at the *New York Times* Food section, Sam Sifton, Patrick Farrell, and Emily Weinstein, who gave me the assignment to explore the machines in the first place. Neither this cookbook nor the last one would exist without them. So many thanks for this, and for the daily inspiration I get from working with such a terrific group of journalists.

As always, there's my adorable agent, Janis Donnaud, who is consistently ten steps ahead of me in every realm.

The stellar team at Clarkson Potter: Doris Cooper, Lydia O'Brien, Marysarah Quinn, Mark McCauslin, Linnea Knollmueller, Kate Tyler, and Erica Gelbard. I love working with you all.

Our wonderful photographer, Christopher Testani, and his team.

And finally I couldn't have done this without my brilliant recipe tester, Jade Zimmerman, who at this point can read my mind (and find stuff there I didn't even realize I was thinking). And many thanks to Adelaide Mueller and Lily Starbuck, who helped make sure every recipe in this book works perfectly, and makes your life easier and tastier. Because that's the point.

INDEX